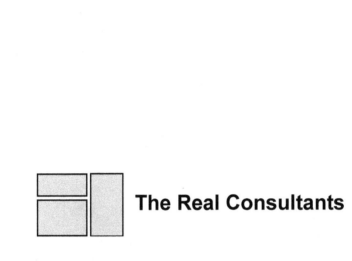 **The Real Consultants**

We empower people to change their lives in a dramatic way for the better!

The Real Consultants LLC
255 Primera Blvd., Suite 160
Lake Mary, FL 32746

Copyright © 2018 by Byron Townsend

All rights reserved, including the right to reproduce this book or portions thereof in any form whatsoever. For information, email CustomerSupport@TheRealConsultantsllc.com.
First The Real Consultant hardcover edition August 2018

For information about special discounts for bulk purchases, please contact The Real Consultants at 1-877-836-7413 or CustomerSupport@TheRealConsultantsllc.com.

Image of Byron on cover: Gabriel Rivera
Editor: Gloria Monahan

The Ten Most Well-Guarded Secrets About Life

A Guide on How to Get You to Where You Want to Be!

Byron B. Townsend, MBA

THE REAL CONSULTANTS LLC | ORLANDO

Table of Contents

About The Book 7
   Who is The Author, Byron Townsend? 7
   What's This Book About? 8
   The Ten Most Well-Guarded Secrets About Life 8

Chapter 1 10
   The "Ignorance is Bliss" Bug 11
   Really, No One Owes You Anything 15
   Take Control, Where Do You Want to Go? 17
   Research, Education, and Mentors 18
   Procrastination, Why Do We All Do It? 20
   Multiple Roads in Life 21
   Attitude Matters, it Really Does! 23
   Psychology, Emotional Intelligence 25
   Your Drive Determines Your Pace 27
   Chapter One Summary – The Driver Seat 28
   Chapter One Action – Where Are You Going? 29

Chapter 2 31
   Time is More Rare than Most Treat It 32
   Time from Now till Death 33
   Always Moving, but Live Life 35
   The Drugs of Time 36
   Current Self vs Future Self 37

A Schedule is the Key	39
Steady Growth	43
Dangerous Paths	44
Opportunities – Don't Miss Your Shot!	46
Chapter Two Summary - Time, a Rare Resource	47
Chapter Two Action – Planned Schedule	49

Chapter 3 52

Introduction	53
Areas of a Budget	54
Monthly Tasks – Debt	55
Monthly Tasks - Credit Cards	56
Monthly Tasks - Forecast	58
Daily & Weekly Budget Tasks	60
More Money Each Year	62
Funds	63
The Plan	64
Saving For Retirement	66
Chapter Three Summary - Money, a Rare Resource	67
Chapter Three Action – Your Budget	69

Chapter 4 73

Introduction	74
Credit Score	74
Financial Stability	78
Managing the Forecast to Feed the Plan	80
The Vision	81

Managing The Risks 82

Managing your Debt 83

Managing your Credit 83

Managing Daily Life 84

Chapter Four Summary – Managing Credit & Financing 84

Chapter Four Actions – The Vision: Your Plan 85

Chapter 5 86

Accomplishing Goals 87

Project Management 88

Short-Term Schedule 89

Relationships 90

External Demeanor 93

Chapter Five Summary - Next Steps in Life, Achieving Goals 95

Chapter Five Action – Short-Term Schedule 96

Final Thoughts 97

A Guide on How to Get You to Where You Want to Be! 98

Recommendation from the Author 99

About The Book

Who is The Author, Byron Townsend?

When Byron was 19, like many others, he was very talented: captain of the track team in high school, Student Senate President, a member of the Army National Guard, first chair cellist, pianist, manager at a large grocery chain, the list goes on. Unfortunately, he was in a terrible car accident shortly after turning 19, losing his right arm and all functionality of his left wrist and fingers – he could only pinch his thumb to the side of his index finger. After a long recovery Byron had an amputated right arm and only a weak pinch on his left hand, he was on the government section 8 housing assistance program, receiving food stamps and disability, with six figures worth of debt knocking at his door. Byron didn't let any of this slow him down; he went on to college to earn multiple degrees, the highest being a master's thus far.

Even with his disability Byron was determined to be independent. To do this he had to be very creative in nearly every situation presented to him - like how could he cook a frozen pizza and not burn himself; or how does he put on a belt or socks with a thumb pinching to the side of his index finger? This constant environment of needing to solve unique, and in many situations, complex scenarios made Byron more patient than most, very skilled at troubleshooting, and great at solving difficult issues. He paired this with the knowledge from his master's degree and decided to design a system to help him accomplish his goals in life. Using the system he created, in just 3 years he doubled nearly tripled his income, was able to pay off more than six figures worth of debt, and now drives a brand new E-Class Mercedes Benz and owns his own business.

Byron began sharing his system with loved ones like friends and family and realized quickly that the system worked for pretty much anyone willing to truthfully follow it. He also feels this knowledge should really be taught to everyone before they graduate high school so we're all better prepared for adulthood. So Byron decided to use his scholarly skills to write a book to teach anyone this system, a way to accomplish one's goals and dreams. So, for those ready for success, but just don't know how to obtain it, check out Byron's book, The Ten Most Well-Guarded Secrets About Life, A Guide on How to Get You to Where You Want to Be!

"Take Control of Your Life, Instead of Letting Life Control What You Can Do!"

-Byron B. Townsend

What's This Book About?

You don't have to live paycheck-to-paycheck forever if you don't want to. Once you learn the keys to success, you decide your path and much of your future! Everyone has many roads they can take through life. Having the right plan and system in place allows you to determine what route you take.

The problem most face is having the time and money to do everything they'd like to do. With so many uncertainties in life how can you take control and ensure you get to where you want to be? This book will teach you, and guide you, as you create the system that will allow you to do just that. You'll learn how to master time management like a professional so you can accomplish all your goals, how to create a budget that ensures your credit score continually rises and you make more money year-over-year, and you'll be guided as you build a system that will take you to where you want to be in life!

The Ten Most Well-Guarded Secrets About Life

As you read through the book you'll learn the ten powerful secrets about life. The table on the next page is to track the page number you find the secrets on, and the secret. As you come back to this guide while building your system for success, this will allow you to quickly locate topics/secrets to reference. So remember each time you locate one of the ten secrets throughout the book, come back to this table to collect them all in one location.

Secret #	Page Found	Details of Secret
#1		
#2		
#3		
#4		
#5		
#6		
#7		
#8		
#9		
#10		

Chapter 1

The Driver Seat

"You don't have to see the whole staircase, just take the first step."

-Martin Luther King Jr.

The "Ignorance is Bliss" Bug

Who Should Read This Book?

If you're a person that doesn't know how to get to where you want to be in life, say by age 30, 40, or 50, then how can you logically or realistically think you'll get there? If you've ever had a goal, objective, dream, or job you wanted, but didn't know how to get there, then this book is for you. Most of us have heard someone successful say you can be whatever you want to be, or do whatever you put your mind to. And if most of you are like I once was you scoff at those statements, like easy to say, but how?! In this book we'll start there, by explaining how you can become anything you set your mind to, within reason, and we'll teach you the topics and skills required to manage the system you'll need to build in order to be successful. These approaches have been tried, tested, and have directly improved my personal skills, self-confidence, and tripled my income in a short period of time. But as you'll learn, whether you succeed or not is ultimately up to if you sincerely want what you want.

We're going to start off by talking about the bug we're all born with, the "ignorance is bliss" bug. We're all born not knowing how the world works, why we feel the way we do, how we succeed in an ever-changing environment. As kids we are ignorant to the fact we live in a society where we need a job to make money and money for the necessities in life such as food and shelter. As children we are ignorant to most things adults must be concerned about on a daily basis, and as a result we become accustomed to our parents taking care of us. Most of you may already know that as humans we are creatures of habit. As kids we all start off life with the "ignorance is bliss" bug. Which simply put, means we are not concerned with many things in life until we become made aware that we should monitor and worry about those things. As children grow older into teens they start learning responsibility and many parents begin attempting to teach their children how to be an adult, and support themselves. However, parents can only teach from their own experience and education. As such, in some cases not every child is given all the key details one needs to be successful in life – and in many cases the child simply wasn't listening to the parent if details were given. Granted, we all learn some details in school and much on our own journey, but you need to understand the big picture across all the different phases of your life to accelerate in life. So, let's segue there, to life phases.

Throughout life there are many phases we'll go through. A phase typically stretches from a time period of 2-5 years. For some folks they may stay stuck, not growing or accomplishing many goals from one phase to the next. However, for those with dreams or plans, people who want to get somewhere in life, they typically see positive changes between the different phases in life. We're going to walk through a few typical phases that hopefully most of you can relate to: One, high school drop outs; Two, high school graduates; Three, people currently in college; Four, Individuals with college degrees.

"You must know where you want to be, to know how to get there quickly."

Life Phase: *No High School Diploma*

Without a high school diploma you can still make it. Some may tell you differently, but you can. That being said, your life will be filled with struggles, risks, and uncertainty, which typically leads to unhappiness and or depression. The later you progress through life the harder it will become, especially if you're single or alone. Most people who are in this phase, past high school graduation age without a GED, fall into one of two buckets: One, you're too busy with life to complete your education; or two, you're too scared or just don't know the steps to obtain your GED. For the first group, those with busy lives, analyze what you do in your life. After eliminating all the important items such as taking care of kids or siblings, working, taking care of the home, etc., what is left? That little bit is all it takes. I get there are genuine obstacles, like dire circumstances that can prevent someone from continuing education. But more times than not the "ignorance is bliss" bug makes it difficult for many to see the bigger picture, the long-term view. Occasionally, it takes help from others to be able to see the long-term view. The day you make the choice you want to succeed in life and get rid of all the stress and risks associated with not having a high school diploma, that's the day you'll fall into the second bucket, i.e., those too scared or just don't know the steps to obtain a GED. For this group, there are many free resources available online to help you through the process.

Life Phase: *High School Graduate*

In the previous life phase, we introduce one of many issues you'll face throughout life, i.e., you're too busy with life to complete your life goals. If this is you, and you skipped reading the previous phase, I strongly advise you to go back and read it. This is a hurdle you'll have to fight with often, and we'll cover how to do that thoroughly in chapter two. Most individuals in the "high school graduate" life phase fall into one of two buckets as it relates to their future. For those who still have a strong "ignorance is bliss" bug, they will not proceed to college. This is perfectly fine if you want to do a trade that doesn't require much education. Some trades require little to no education to pursue. Many are admirable trades that not just anyone can do, they require specific skills. Before you decide to follow these paths ask yourself three questions: Is it realistic that you will achieve your goal that requires little to no education? Are you OK making the level of money this particular trade pays when you're 30, 40, and 50? And are you OK still working in this trade until you retire? Think about these questions hard, and be real with yourself! If you sincerely can't easily say "Yes!" to all of these questions then you should join the second group of folks in this phase of their life – or be OK with knowing you're going down a dangerous path, and we'll talk about dangerous paths later in this chapter.

The second bucket of folks in this phase of their life knows in order to get to where they want to go they'll need some education. However, many don't know how to start down the path of going to college. For some they don't know what they want to be. Many folks feel they can't afford it. Some feel they aren't smart enough, or their high school grades were too low. Trust me, if you continue to let these fears stop you from accomplishing your goals, you will start making that a default in life – which isn't good. Below are a few fears many folks face when thinking of attending college:

- **College is Too Expensive** – Community College, work study, and financial aid solves this for nearly anyone. In today's world it's a common reality that most individuals can't afford college. With the mixture of Federal support/aid, scholarship opportunities, and flexible scheduling options, college can be a reality for students who are serious about obtaining a degree.
- **My High School Grades Were Horrible** - Community college doesn't care if your grades aren't great; they'll let you attend. As it relates to grades,

community college is like a second chance if you had poor grades in high school.
- **I Don't Know What I Want to Do** – Being blunt, most people—even those in their thirties and forties—don't really feel like they know what they want to do with their life. A college degree allows you to float around on a degree and make some money while figuring out your dreams and sorting out the details/niche. In chapter six we'll go through an exercise to help you figure out what you want to be, or do in your future.

"You must know where you want to be, to know how to get there."

Life Phase: *College Students*

Many college students feel because they're in college they're on the right path, or a path. In reality, that's not necessarily true. Life is a combination of experience and education, with experience having much more of an impact. What that means is even though you're in college, if you're not getting experience in the right areas then you're taking the long road to your destination. None of us are immortal, so why would you choose the longer path? College students should really understand where they want to be in life, three to five years from now. Knowing this they can begin to identify what jobs they'll need, and that's critical. With that, you now know all the educational requirements and skills needed for the jobs you want in the future; In short, the requirements to get you to where you want to be in life from a career/job perspective. In addition, for anyone in debt, being in college is a great way to solve your debt issues. But we'll get into that in chapter three. For now, let's take a look at the finale life phase example.

Life Phase: *College Graduates*

People who fall into this phase can learn a lot from this book. Granted, anyone in an earlier phase of their life prior to college graduation can definitely get into, and through, college by following the instructions in this book. However, this book really starts to help excel folks who have obtained a degree. I feel college graduates need the most assistance because there are less materials available to help them quickly get to the next level and beyond. Many college graduates feel because they've accomplished the task of getting a college degree that everything will work out. The promotions and jobs will just come to them because they have a degree. Many college graduates are shocked to find that reality doesn't match that vision for the vast majority of people. All a college degree gives you is the ability to cross that requirement off your long list of requirements to get you to where you want to be. You still have to prove you can apply that knowledge, earn the job you want, and get more experience. Getting your degree simply means you've gone up a few floors in the skyscraper of life.

The Skyscraper of Life

The skyscraper is an analogy I use to describe the different phases in growth a person travels throughout life. We all start out on the first floor of the skyscraper when we're born. As we grow older and get more experience and education in life, we start to obtain wisdom and move up floors within the skyscraper. If we look at the life phases discussed previously they all have the same two things in common that all phases share. They all are ignorant to something, meaning there are many more floors in their skyscraper for them to climb. And second, until a person gets rid of their "ignorance is bliss" bug, it's going to be difficult for them to steer their life in the right direction to get to where they want to be. You are in the driver seat of your life. Figure out where you're driving to so you can begin climbing up the multitude of floors in the skyscraper of life. Don't be that person at 40, 50, or 60, asking why you didn't achieve your dreams, asking how you got to where you are. You're behind the wheel; navigate life to get the skills and education you need to get to where you want to go. But how do you do this?

Really, No One Owes You Anything

Luck, The Objective State

There are many ways to get to where you want to go in life, once you know where you want to go – which in itself can be difficult to accomplish. However, due to the fact we're all born with the "ignorance is bliss" bug, there's a misconception that many people have. Most people subconsciously feel like someone owes them something. Some individuals, in many phases of their life, don't feel they need a plan for life. They think, "I'll marry someone well off." Or, "I'll win the lottery." They're not quite sure how they'll reach their goals, but they know something lucky will happen in their life to get them there. What they fail to realize is that luck, good or bad, is completely outside of one's control; therefore, no one can blame themselves for not being lucky or take any pride in their good luck. In short, if you fall into this bucket of thinking, that you'll get lucky and life will work out, there's a high probability things will not work out as you've planned.

Everything Will Work Out

For successful people they hear this phrase a lot (i.e., everything will work out). Typically, because either they know, or they have people around them supporting them who know, you must plan and prepare in order to accomplish goals and live your dreams. Unfortunately, most of us don't plan and schedule key areas of our life, yet we still subconsciously feel as if everything will work out. It's because of the "ignorance is bliss" bug. Once you have a plan to reach your achievements, you can accomplish your goals, and live your dreams. When you get on this path, then everything will work out. Until then, ensure you have a high-level plan or idea – or think about it.

"Don't expect some magical event, rich significant other, or luck will get you where you want to be; no one owes you anything!"

I Know What I Want to Do, but Don't Know How to Get There

Like I mentioned before, you have to have some idea where you want to be in three to five years from now, at a high-level. For example, do you want to be a manager, promoted to a specific rank, be proficient in something, buy a house, have a child, or acquire degrees? When you close your eyes and envision who you want to be five years from now, start jotting down some notes. Do this exercise every day for a few weeks. Share your list with close friends, family, people who will keep it real with you. You need people who will tell you if your vision is not realistic. We'll also cover in detail how to thoroughly create realistic and achievable goals in chapter six.

Once you know what you want to do, the next steps are simple. You must draft out your high-level plan to get to where you want to go, a long-term schedule. First, before we even go there, I know many of you are thinking it's not that simple; it can't be. Let's first talk about why you feel that way, and how to get over that hump so you can be successful with your plan.

Take Control, Where Do You Want to Go?

Stop Playing the Victim Due to Your Ignorance

Many people experience this phenomenon in their life, or know someone who has. Where you feel like once things start going great, something always goes wrong. It's called Murphy's Law. If you've experienced this multiple times in your life it's more than likely due to one of two reasons. Either one, something out of your control has occurred, e.g., if a loved one passes, or a hurricane hits your home, something out of your control. The second are things that we can control, or plan for. Things we can control simply need to be managed accordingly. These are called short term risks. The point I'm trying to make is if it's a controllable risk, the only reason it's negatively affecting you is because you still have the "ignorance is bliss" bug and probably think some short-term risks are actually items out of your control. This is an easy mistake to make. If you're unsure if a risk is in or out of your control, one technique to determine this is to ask yourself: If you had $25,000, would that issue matter? If the answer is no, no amount of money could solve this dilemma, then it's out of your control. If you answer yes, more money would solve this dilemma, then you need to better understand what a short-term risk is.

"Do you ever feel like once you catch a break, something bad always happens?"

Manage Your Short-Term Risks

So, what is a short-term risk specifically? It's an aspect about your life that you need, or will need, but may not have the resources for. For example, gasoline is one. Do you know anyone who has ever worried about gas money, or has needed gas money, or even worse, has run out of gas? That's someone not managing their short-term risks. Pet food, money for a haircut, medical or car maintenance expenses, etc. are all items we need. So, if you haven't planned and managed to have resources for those events, then there's a short-term risk you're choosing to ignore. Some of you may say, "I'm not ignoring it, I can't afford it!" That may be true, but there are a few things you can do to better manage your short-term risks. In chapter three we'll go through exercises to help you manage your short-term risks. Don't be the person always complaining; Instead, use that time to do something about the situation.

> "If you don't take control of your life, crying about it isn't going to make it any better!"

Don't Complain, Take Control

So, what have you learned thus far? There are things in this world out of our control. If you get knocked down, you're the only one in the driver seat that can decide to get back up. For everything else, accept the fact that you have the "ignorance is bliss" bug. Stop complaining, take control, and learn what you need to learn to manage your short-term risks. In chapter two and three we'll talk about the system you can put in place to manage your short-term risks, if you're in the mindset to grow. Other than this book, there may be other resources needed to build your system to navigate up the skyscraper of life.

Research, Education, and Mentors

Research

When I was growing up information had to be sought after by going to the library and reading a book. Today, information is not only free, it's easily accessible. I simply say, "OK Google," to my smart phone and ask any question. I'm quickly presented with my answer. What this means is there's really no excuse for not being able to understand the steps you'll need to take to get you to where you want to be in life. Granted, not everyone may have a smart phone, or even a computer and internet. However, most cities still have a library which offers computers and internet. Some of you may need to gain the knowledge the old fashion way, by heading to the library. The point is you'll want to use research to look up different roles, positions you'll need to fill, to get you to where you want to be. But I know you're saying, "What if I'm not sure what I want to be," right? We'll cover that as well.

> How do you plan to learn the skills needed, get the experience required, or obtain the job to get your foot in the door for the life you want?

Education

Education is needed for most well-paying stable jobs. It may only be for a few months such as professions like a hair stylist, or it may be many years as is the case to become a doctor or lawyer. If you're unsure what you want to be, that's fine. However, life keeps moving forward and the longer you sit idle, the longer you won't be moving towards a goal. Looking at what classes your local colleges offer may spark some interests. Find a few classes or a program that looks interesting to you and read it over in detail, take a class. In chapter seven we'll do a deep dive into how you can get started with college, and the hurdles to watch out for. However, most people don't know what they want to be because they're not entirely sure what each job entails – at least not well enough to know if it's something they want to do for the rest of their lives. That's where mentors come in. And colleges are a great place to find a mentor.

"To get to where you want to be, you'll probably need to grow!"

Mentors

A mentor is someone you trust, that has more knowledge and experience than you, and can advise you on one or multiple topics. A mentor is an absolute necessity. It's simple, we can all learn the easy way via research, education, and a mentor, or we can learn the hard way, through experience. Some of us, like me, are stubborn and must unfortunately learn many things the hard way. This is not a bright approach the majority of the time. You'll fall, scrape your knees, and struggle in many occasions, taking much longer than desired to accomplish a task. A mentor informs you the way they took, what they learned, and some things to look out for so you can get it right the first time. Of course there are many things you'll still need to learn through experience. Mentors help you navigate your way up the skyscraper of life by telling you all their secrets they've learned in life, to help get you where you want to be quicker. Even knowing this, many people procrastinate and involuntarily struggle to follow the sound advice. Procrastination has a way of making many of us do things against our better judgment. As such, it will make many of you reading this now not follow through with taking action, even when the steps to success are handed to you in black and white. So next we're going to cover why this phenomenon called procrastination affects so many of us and how you can overcome it to be successful with this guide.

Procrastination, Why Do We All Do It?

Procrastination

Procrastination, put simply, is postponing a task, typically because it's something you don't want to do and often against better judgement. Summed up, you're choosing to have your future-self deal with the task or issue – as if your future-self will want to deal with the task or issue any more than you do today. The consequence of procrastination, long-term, can be very bad, preventing you from capitalizing on opportunities and achieving your goals. As humans we are creatures of habit. Meaning if you procrastinate a lot, you will habitually continue to do so. Procrastination in our skyscraper of life is locked doors. In short, the more you procrastinate the harder it is traveling through the skyscrapers' floors to get to the next level. Most people know much of what I mentioned; so why do they continue to procrastinate? The main reason is because we're human, and most of us will procrastinate no matter what. However, if we know this, then we are empowered to identify it when it's occurring. That is the key. When you notice you're procrastinating, do something about it. This is one half of the solution. Having the ability to identify when you're procrastinating is very important, but on top of that you'll need a structure to manage procrastination.

How do you procrastinate?

No Structure with Deadlines

Ultimately there are two things everyone needs to know to not procrastinate. The first is the ability to accept the fact that you procrastinate and identify when it's occurring. You can research many methods on how to identify if you're procrastinating, and we'll cover many in chapter two. The second is having a structure. Think about it, most people go to work, right? They show up on time, without procrastination getting in the way – the majority of the time. What's the difference between the goal to go to work and a life goal? It's simple; work has a structured schedule for you to follow and consequences. That's exactly what you need in your personal life to help put deadlines on life goals and manage procrastination. A schedule will add structure to your life and allow you to look at issues and goals in smaller pieces.

Another major reason why people procrastinate is because of laziness and the fear of failure. Only self-control can conquer the laziness, but the fear is fueled by trying to look at the task or issue as a whole. That's like looking at an elephant and being told, wash it, you have half an hour. That's overwhelming, like what, how!? However, if you took time before you started to section off parts of the elephant, make a schedule of which sections you'll tackle when, then you're only looking at small sections and not the whole elephant. This approach helps you manage your fear and get over procrastination.

"Being productive on other tasks as a way to avoid a particular task is a form of procrastination."

Focus, Staying Busy Doesn't Mean You're Not Procrastinating
Procrastination can be tricky, even for those who stay productive. Many people procrastinate when it comes to accomplishing unpleasant tasks. One method of doing so is by staying busy doing many other tasks on your to-do list, but avoiding the one task you don't want to complete. You have to be careful not to fall for this tricky form of procrastination. Again, in chapter two we'll cover how to manage procrastination via a schedule. It's much easier to have the self-confidence to defeat procrastination when you have a schedule and know which path you want to travel up the skyscraper. We've been concentrating on barriers that may make it difficult to grow and travel up the skyscraper of life. Now, let's shift gears a bit to talk about the multiple paths or roads you have on your way up the skyscraper.

Multiple Roads in Life

The Roads of Life
There are multiple paths up the massive skyscraper of life, with many other people trying to travel up the various paths with you. So what are the paths on the road of life? Put simply, they are the road from where you are today, to where you'll end up in life later. Some people are on dangerous paths. These are paths whereby if they don't change something significant in their life they'll end up in jail, homeless, or dead. For individuals on this path

they typically need a traumatic event in their life to get them to realize the path they're on.

In the polar opposite spectrum, many people in college or with college degrees start down their paths, but due to the "ignorance is bliss" bug they forget they're in the driver seat. They forget it's imperative to supplement their education if they want to continue moving up the skyscraper of life. Otherwise you'll become stagnate, no longer traveling down your path, but instead remaining in the same state from phase to phase. This is fine when you've reached your goal on where you want to be in life, and are positioned to achieve your dreams. However, if you have bigger plans, and want to achieve more, you must drive further.

"Everyone has many roads they can take through life; smart ones choose their path."

Experience

As stated before, education is needed for those wanting to make some good money in life (e.g., more than $70 thousand a year). However, to truthfully excel you must be able to understand your education well enough to apply it, and you must understand it needs to be supplemented with experience. That last part is a very important key. When you graduate from college, if you don't have the right experience then you'll take much longer to get to where you want to be. What that means is, if by 30 you want to be a front desk manager in a hotel, and by 40 the general manager of a nice hotel, then you had better be working at a hotel and getting experience in the industry as you're in college. This is why it's important to think about what you want to be, or where you want to be in the future. It helps you understand what industry you should begin getting experience in immediately. The industry is the driving factor; you don't have to be working the specific role you want in the future while in college, you just simply need to be in the appropriate industry.

What road do you want to travel in your life? Where do you want to go?

Certifications

Once you're working in your industry and you get your degree, you're not done. Now it's time to understand what certificates are available for your industry. For example, if you love multitasking and managing complex projects, maybe you'll want to become a Project Manager. There's a certificate called the Project Management Certificate (PMP) that is known in the Project Management community as the certificate saying you know what you're doing. By simply studying for a few months and taking a test, you'll now be worth a lot more money, simply because you got a certificate in your industry. Be smart about how you choose your path so you can get to where you want to be much quicker. However, even knowing everything I've shared thus far some of you still won't finish this book. For those that do, a subset of you won't actually follow through with getting to where you want to be in the skyscraper of life. Why? Simply put, you don't have the right attitude, period!

Attitude Matters, it Really Does!

Attitude Can Drive Unwanted Actions

Attitude is an emotion, and like all emotions it can control your actions. That's impeccably important so I'm going to repeat that. Emotions can control your actions, and many times when they do it is against your best interests. Think about it. Anger, jealousy, and depression are all emotions that when pushed to their extremes will push a person to kill another individual or commit suicide. This is emotion forcibly controlling someone's actions. Attitude is as equally as powerful as the emotions mentioned above. Our environment growing up has a lot to do with what shapes our attitude. For example, some people with rough upbringings may be perceived by others as "ratchet," or not as classy. Because attitude can affect how you're perceived, it has a huge impact on how successful you are in the driver seat of your life. In short, if you hate your job you need to realize you're not on the path you want to be on. Don't have a negative attitude about life, do something about life and get on a different path. And every path will have difficulties. Just remember, you need to control your attitude.

> "Negativity will bring negativity via the law of attraction; Just as positivity will bring positivity!"

Close Minded, People Are Not Out to Get You

Before we talk about how to control your attitude, you first must understand something about life. Because everyone is on a different floor on the skyscraper of life, different people around you may have the "ignorance is bliss" bug more than you. Meaning, they may not understand the world as much as you; maybe they haven't had as much experience or education. The point being, they may not be as knowledgeable. As such, they may rub you the wrong way, may annoy you, or may inadvertently cause you to have a negative attitude. At these times you need to stop, realize the emotion of attitude is trying to control your actions, and tell yourself this person isn't out to get me. They just don't realize from my perspective how annoying or stupid they're being. I promise, the majority of these folks are not out to get you. When you learn to control your attitude, take a deep breath, and take yourself off that ledge, you're then in control to better analyze the situation and outsmart others – or take the best approach for you. As a result, you will travel up the skyscraper of life much faster than your competition on the same path as you. The key takeaway from this section is to stop feeling like someone's out to get you, and realize there are multiple perspectives to every situation.

When your morning starts off terrible, doesn't that leave a nasty stain on the day?

There are Multiple Perspectives, Don't Judge, Simply Understand

As stated before, in most circumstances that provoke negative attitudes, if you can stop and just recognize that's what's happening, then you've graduated to being able to better manage and control your attitude. To get to this point you must first start with trying to at least notice when you're starting to have a bad attitude – for me this is any morning I have to get up really early☺. Once you can identify you're having a grumpy or bad attitude, there are many exercises to help you cope with the attitude, then control it. In all the exercises you must realize that based on many variables, there will always be multiple perspectives to most situations. My favorite exercise to manage negative attitude is to tell myself, "Today's going to be a great day!!" Every morning when something negative happens that makes me start to feel a negative attitude, I simply say out loud, "Today's going to be a great day!!" And saying it out loud is a key part, and notice the two exclamation marks. Why do this? Why continue to say out loud, "Today's going to be a great day!!" when I begin to feel a negative attitude? You probably already know the answer. As humans we are creatures of habit. After a while, two things will happen. First, you'll get better at identifying when something triggers you to have a negative attitude. And secondly, you will actually start believing that today will be a great day. Sincerely, try it for a week. Every morning, when anything brings negativity to you, say out loud that "Today's going to be a great day!!" Now for those of you with this issue with other emotions, you may be thinking what exercises can you use for those? The answer is simple, understand emotional intelligence.

Psychology, Emotional Intelligence

Emotional Intelligence

So, what is emotional intelligence? It's something I feel everyone should be required to learn in high school, in-depth. Emotional intelligence is the ability to understand and manage emotions, yours and others. Remember, emotions when not managed can control your actions – and in many situations in a negative way. **For this reason, this is the first of the ten well-guarded secrets about life; you must learn emotional intelligence *very* well if you want to be successful in life.** The great thing about emotional intelligence is the fact that it's a learnable skill. Meaning it's not just something you're born with or not born with; you can learn it. Having the ability to understand emotions well enough to manage your own should be on everyone's goal list. The sooner you learn this skill, the faster you'll be able to get to where you're headed to in the skyscraper of life.

"Emotional Intelligence is one of many skills found in all great leaders and successful individuals."

Emotional Control

There are two areas around emotional intelligence you must master before you can better manage your emotions. Also keep in mind, traumatic events such as a close loved one passing will always tug on your emotions; and you're not meant to control your emotions at those times – you should be grieving. I'm referring to your average day, everyday life. The first area is emotional awareness. You need to understand what the various types of emotions are, and be able to identify when you're expressing them. You can research to identify the various emotions, and how people typically express them. I recommend starting off with the top 8 most common emotions (i.e., fear, anger, sadness, joy, disgust, trust, anticipation/anxious, and surprise). Once you've improved at identifying when you're expressing a specific emotion, you'll naturally begin to read others' emotions much better.

Once you can recognize when emotions are driving action, or are occurring, you're ready to move to the second area, being able to use emotions. What I mean by this is the ability to apply emotions to tasks like problem solving or thinking. For example, if you've observed a specific series of events causes your significant other to get upset, but you absolutely feel you need to do those specific series of events anyways, you might want to do them at a time when it's OK for your significant other to *not* be happy – for example don't do it during a gift-giving holiday if you want gifts. That would be using emotional intelligence to help drive thinking and problem solving. Now many of you are probably thinking, well that example is common sense and you'd be 100% correct for most people who have reached a specific floor in the skyscraper of life. But if everyone was on that same level in the skyscraper then less men would be in the dog house. ☺ Once you've mastered being aware of your own emotions and applying emotional intelligence to thinking, you're ready to manage your emotions.

"Do you have emotional intelligence or do you need to learn this skill?"

Managing Emotions

Now for many of you, you're thinking "once I master blah blah, what are you talking about!! How do I master my emotions!?" Like I said, this is a skill. And like great pianists, great leaders, or great athletes, they'll all tell you they didn't get great until after many years of practice and many failures. Emotional intelligence is a skill you can't expect to learn in a few years. It may take 5-10 years to get half way decent at managing your emotions. The point being you must first be aware that you can learn this skill before you'll start down that path. Once you've learned how to manage your emotions you'll be able to regulate your own to adapt for the various situations you'll face on your path up the skyscraper of life.

Your Drive Determines Your Pace

Find a Motivator to Succeed

You are in the driver seat of your life. But one important factor to understand is that you're walking through the skyscraper. The more drive you have, the more you want your goals, the quicker you want to get to your destination, the faster you'll walk and the quicker you'll get there. Now some of you are a diamond in the rough. What does that mean exactly? It means, of all the character traits that make up successful people, you've got some naturally that are hard to learn. For example, many of you reading this today know you're not exactly where you'd like to be in life. You all have a trait of a diamond in the rough because you're doing something about it by reading up on how to grow. Accepting you are not where you want to be and taking action is one of the traits needed to be considered a diamond in the rough. For those of you who think a lot of the emotional intelligence stuff we covered is common sense, it's because you possess that skill to some degree, giving you a trait of a diamond in the rough. The flip side to a diamond in the rough is that you are not polished. Yes a diamond in the rough may have some skills naturally that are hard to learn, but they're still missing tons of experience and education. Smart diamonds in the rough use this advantage to excel through the skyscraper of life more quickly Again, if you've reached your destination, or prefer a slower approach to your goals, that's totally a route you can take as you're the driver. Despite whether you're a diamond in the rough or not, you must figure out what will motivate you to keep moving through the skyscraper.

What motivates you, and what are the things that will drive you to success?

If you have the drive, what's the next step?

At this point some of you are saying OK I get it. You know you have to make some changes in your life, you just don't know how. The point of this chapter was to open your eyes to the reason successful people say you can be whatever you want to be, or do whatever you put your mind to. They say this because it's true. You're in the driver seat so you determine if you do any of your goals or dreams in life. For those of you ready to start taking control of what path you're on in life, continue on in this book, starting with reading the summary of this chapter thoroughly. If you're not ready to take charge, save yourself the time and put this book down; it's only for people ready to take control of their life and learn how to get to where they want to be in life.

Chapter One Summary – The Driver Seat

This chapter has some powerful content in it. I'm hoping you learned you're in the driver seat of your life, and that you have the "ignorance is bliss" bug – we all do. Knowing this allows you to understand no one owes you anything. If you don't like the fact you're ignorant, you have to take control and figure out where you want to go in life or who you want to be. If you're like most individuals and have no clue, research, take some classes in an industry that interests you, or find a mentor and ask them, learn from them. The point is you're driving. Don't let procrastination cause you to sit stagnant from one phase of your life to the next. You should be growing, heading towards your goals and dreams. For you to get there you've got to fully understand **the second most well-guarded secret about life; you're in the driver seat.**

Remember there are multiple roads to get to where you want to be in life. Knowing this, be sure you know what path you're currently on. Is it the one you want to be on? If not, why are you on it, you're the driver? As you're traveling your paths know that your attitude matters, as well as your ability to learn emotional intelligence well, the first well-guarded secret. In the end, you're walking through the skyscraper of life. The purpose of this chapter is to make you aware that if you're not where you want to be, it's because you haven't decided to go someplace else. Throughout this book we'll give you the structure and system to empower you to pick a path in life, plan it out, and start full speed up the skyscraper to get you to where you want to be in life. In the next chapter you'll learn how to locate the shortcuts in the skyscraper of life – to really get moving. Once you've decided enough is enough and you're ready to accomplish your goals, you're the one taking yourself wherever you're willing to go.

"I can put the food up to the horse's mouth but I can't force him to eat it."

Chapter One Action – Where Are You Going?

Each chapter teaches one or two of the well-guarded secrets about life. However, knowing about them is only half the battle. You must be able to apply them if you're going to get anywhere. This is where most fail; they talk the talk and get it, but do nothing to follow-through! Your required action from chapter one is to fill out the below table. What I mean by required is you'll have a lot of trouble locating the shortcuts in the skyscraper of life, which is taught in chapter two, if you don't have the below table figured out. The table you're being asked to populate has columns showing you current state, three years from now, and six years from now. Each row represents an aspect of your life. Complete the table by starting with your current state – where you are today in life for each category, then where you want to be three and six years from now. Share your list with close friends, family, people who will keep it real with you. If you're uncertain how to populate, look at the example and definitions provided.

Action Row Definitions
- Education – This is formal education at an institution – in person or virtual – towards a degree or certificate
- Career – This is the title in your career you'd like to be. Remember, the industry you want to be in is the key; starting there you can research/Google to identify what positions in that industry may interest you.
- Personal Growth – This is areas where you'd like to grow outside of formal education. For example, this may be learning how to do your own oil change or learning a foreign language. What do you not know today, that you'd like to know in the future?
- Physical Growth – What physical activity goals do you have? If none, that should change.
- Standard of Living – This really focuses on the type of living situation that you would like ideally (e.g., having roommates or not, renting a one or two bedroom apt., buying a house, etc.). In addition, it looks at the type of vehicle, love life, number of vacations, massages monthly, whatever you'd like your standard of living to be, this is where it goes.

Fill out the empty fields.

Categories	Current	3 Years From Now	6 Years From Now
Education			
Career			
Personal Growth			
Physical Growth			
Standard of Living			

The Example

Categories	Current	3 Years From Now	6 Years From Now
Education	Working on Associates Degree	Obtained Bachelors	Obtain Masters
Career	Server	Working Front Desk at Hotel	Front Desk Manager on way to Assistant General Manager
Personal Growth	Home Maker	Obtain Hotel Industry Certification	Learn all areas of a hotel and Spanish
Physical Growth	Sporadic Exercise	Consistent Working out	Run a 5K event each year
Standard of Living	New Corolla, 3BR apt.	New Honda Accord, 3 BR apt.	New Lexus, new house

Chapter 2

Time, a Rare Resource

"Don't count the days, make the days count."

- Muhammad Ali

Time is More Rare than Most Treat It

It's Finite

In chapter one you learned you're in the driver seat, so you must take yourself to where you want to go in life. You also learned that you must research and grow your emotional intelligence skills. If you're truthfully and sincerely ready to accomplish your goals and dreams, then you also completed the Action section of chapter one and have some high-level idea where you're trying to get to in the skyscraper of life. In this chapter we're going to look at one of the most precious and rare resources in life, time. Time is finite, meaning it has limits or boundaries. As such, you must treat it as more precious than gold. However, most people don't even track or manage time. Many of us take the time to budget and track how we spend our money, but very few track how their time is spent – as if it's unlimited. Sure, we know we may sleep 5-8 hours a night, and may work 30-50 hours a week. But how much time do you spend socializing, working out, self-learning, attending school, doing homework, home chores, hobbies, relaxing, etc.? Once you're a self-sufficient adult fully supporting yourself there's a lot to do – you'll soon miss the days when you had enough free time to say "I'm bored." However, if you're attempting to get somewhere in life you have to determine when you'll get the necessary tasks completed to get you there. To do that, you must learn time management, very well.

"How you spend your time determines how much you'll get out of life."

Time Management

Many individuals feel like they know what time management is and that they possess that skill. However, if you're not a person who accomplishes goals, consistently, then you do not possess good time management skills. Time management is the ability to plan and control how you spend your time each day to effectively accomplish your goals. So, to be successful in the driver seat you must master time management. The great thing about time management is that it is a skill that you can learn and get really good at. In this chapter we'll give you the background and teach you a system to effectively manage your time, allowing you to accomplish your goals to get you to where you want to be.

Time has No Take Backs

With time you get no take backs; you can't travel back in time – at least not today as far as I'm aware. So, if you make the decision to switch life paths and begin traveling down a new route, you have to learn, grow, or gain something from the time you spent on that first path. For some they can say in the past 6 months I've grown and learned a lot through experiences. Others can say the same, but in addition they can also say during that time they've obtained many key objectives towards their goals – and you should fall in the latter bucket. In the driver seat today, if you can't say confidently **what** you want to accomplish in your life - on your current path - during the next 6 months, then there's a high probability you're wasting time. The point of this section is you can't get time back. Don't waste it! Try to be productive and proactive about obtaining your goals, daily.

Time from Now till Death

Live Life

Before introducing you to the system you can use to effectively manage your time, let's first discuss some background around this rare resource. There are three areas of time we'll discuss: Its short life span and the need to view it from a high-level; the calculation to the right work/life balance; and the drugs of time. As life is what you make it, it's important to ensure you have that mindset. You have to ask yourself what you want to do in life, and write these things down – as we started to do in the chapter one action exercise. This will help you throughout life, but more specifically when you get to chapter 6 and we map out the blueprints to your long-term goals they will be very helpful.

What would you do if you knew you had 80 years to live?

Accomplish Your Goals

Throughout life everyone has goals, achievements or objectives they want to attain. Depending on how you do in accomplishing current goals, you reset what goals you have, and move forward on accomplishing new ones. Time is the pathway to those accomplishments. If time is managed, you'll reach your destination much quicker. However, some goals have a lot of requirements and may take many years to accomplish. As such, it's important to view time from a high-level, realizing we only exist for a very short period on earth. If you could only live 80 years, when do you want to retire to just enjoy life? What job(s) would you want to do throughout your life, what industry and career? What size house do you want? Do you want kids? Will your parents have money for nursing homes, or will you need to support them? Many things in life will get in the way of you accomplishing goals. This is why it's imperative to remember that the time available in your life is finite; view your life, and time management, from a high-level.

"You can only make so much money from now, until the day you die."

Retire Early

Another area everyone is aware of and knows they must save for, but many wait to do so or never do, is preparation for retirement. When thinking about your life and how you plan to support yourself, you have to accept an important fact that the "ignorance is bliss" bug makes many of us not concerned about until later years in life. And that is that during the very beginning and end of your life you must have some way to support yourself without working. For the vast majority of us we were fortunate enough to have one or two parents to support our early years in life. However, for retirement, we have to siphon a little out each year we work to cover our later years in life. And as retirement is a time when you should be crossing off bucket list items, you want to make sure you can live comfortably without being concerned about money. The point being made is you have to look at your life from a high-level to ensure you're fully covered for your future.

"Don't just look out for the 'you' now, look out for the 'you' in three years, or five!"

Always Moving, but Live Life

Live to Work

In a previous section of this chapter we mentioned the three areas of time we'll be discussing: Its short life span and the need to view it from a high-level; the calculation to the right work/life balance; and the drugs of time. We just covered how we live a short life span and we must view life from a high-level holistically. This is an important aspect about life every successful person knows, and many of you will need to fully grasp, or accept this, in order to become good at time management. Let's now segue into the second of those three topics, the calculation to the right work/life balance. One perspective of all the content shared thus far is, "this guy sounds like every minute of my life should be planned, what about relaxing, hobbies, free time, being spontaneous and living!?" The view of planning out every minute, or even every hour, is extreme. At this end of the extreme we have the workaholics or people who are always busy. Not all, but many of those individuals simply are trying to achieve a goal and working hard in an attempt to reach them. Personally, I find that admirable if done correctly. Otherwise, if not approached a certain way you end up working really hard, burning out, and accomplishing very little. The point being made is that different people have different drives. If you're more of a workaholic type, that's fine and you'll probably excel through the skyscraper. Just make sure you're working hard on the right tasks in the right order to achieve your goals and live. For the people on the other end of the spectrum, more on the, "I don't really like this thing called work" side of the fence, let's talk about what that does to your life, at a high-level.

Work to Live

For the individuals who find they often say, I'm bored." Or people who slowly work on objectives in life. That is absolutely and entirely a path available for you to take. If you want to barely work and coast by chilling, you can. There are even government programs to assist you. The great thing about understanding you're in the driver seat means you can switch paths at any time to start traveling a new one. But coasting through life with no plan can be dangerous. As we are habitual creatures, the longer you stay on a path the harder it is to leave it. And unfortunately, this path is plagued with risks, uncertainty, and struggles. Definitely more so as you age and approach retirement with no plan. Now I'm not saying you can't relax and chill in life. The point is there's a balance. That balance varies for everyone.

The Balance

So, what is that calculation, that happy medium between working nonstop and barely working, the work/life balance? That is defined by two things: the dreams and goals you want, and what you're willing to do to achieve them. If you want to be the President of the United States, then I'd say you have to be OK with a dominantly working life with little free time. If you want to be a front desk manager for a nice hotel chain, you have more chill time in your life. You'll still need to put in some years working, college will help. Again, how much time you should invest working depends on what your goals in life are. And if you're not willing to do what it takes to achieve your goals, then be realistic with yourself and lower your standards/goals. Otherwise you're simply setting yourself up for failure, over and over again. It's OK to have smaller goals then grow them. Later in this chapter, we'll talk about how you decide what the best goals are for your drive.

The Drugs of Time

The Everyday Drug

So, of the three areas discussed we covered how we live a short life span and must view life high-level to thoroughly plan for it. And most recently we discussed the importance of knowing your life goals and drive to determine a good work/life balance. In this section we'll be covering the drugs of time. That's right, time has many drugs. To level set, a drug is something which has a physiological effect when ingested or otherwise introduced to the body. For time, this is anything that drains a lot of time when not needed. For example, have you ever heard of video games or TV? I'm not saying you can't watch TV or play video games. On the contrary, I love to game. We need relax and have down time. What I'm saying is if today your goals were to work out before work, go to work, get a haircut after work, and file your taxes, then you probably shouldn't make the decision to watch TV or play video games that evening until all those tasks are complete. Again, anything that slows you down or prevents you from accomplishing your daily goals, are drugs to time and can harm your success.

Socializing

The deadliest of drugs to time today is social media. You know what I'm referring to right? I'm talking about the Facebook games or scrolling through your timeline, viewing your friends' Snapchat stories, or Twitter. People don't realize these social media apps are viewed from a time management perspective as social time. Except, many people spend so much time socializing they don't have time to accomplish their objectives or goals in life. Or if they do, it's very slowly with large gaps of time between major accomplishments. If being on social media is intentional and you're OK with where you're at in life, then that's absolutely fine to fill up free time with social media. However, if you're a person trying to get somewhere in life you can't fill your day up with socializing; you've got real shit to do!

"Don't live behind technology watching the world, live your life!"

Scheduling

The purpose of this chapter is to give you background and teach you a system to effectively manage your time, allowing you to accomplish your goals to get you to where you want to be. We've covered the important background you need to understand how to manage time well, that was: we have a short life span and need to view life and time from a high-level; we discussed the importance of knowing your life goals and drive to determine a good work/life balance; and we made you aware of a few drugs to time you must watch out for, and manage. Before we talk about the system to manage your time (i.e., a schedule), let's talk about what time management really is at its core, time administration.

Current Self vs Future Self

Time Administration

So, what do I mean by time administration? It's very simple, every time you make a decision to spend a chunk of your time doing a specific task, you're administering your time, or practicing time management. When we sit down and strategically plan out our time, we are choosing how we want to spend our time, rather than leaving the decision up to our feelings. Remember, earlier we spoke about emotional intelligence and control because if you aren't aware of your emotions, your emotions can often drive your actions – and typically against your best interests. How we're feeling at the time determines what we *feel* like doing at that time. Leaving your time to emotions is the same as leaving your life to chance; you never know how you're going to feel. That's why it's imperative you administer your time strategically, rather than letting your emotions determine what you do.

Financial Debt

So, what is debt relative to time? Debt is something you owe, typically money. When you collect financial debt today, you're stealing from your future self. Some debt is fine. For example, if you get a mortgage for a house you can afford or a vehicle loan within your price range, this is good debt. However, when you get loans or put items on credit cards without money to pay them off quickly, then you're stealing money from your future self. Trust me your future self, three years from now, will be very unhappy that they're paying on your younger self's debt. When you think about building a system to manage your time, you have to recall that part of managing your time is also making sure you're spending it in a way that will not only support you and your family today, but also your future self and family as well. In addition, your system needs to allow you to accomplish your goals and live your dreams. Debt will be a hindrance in getting you to where you want to be. Avoid bad debt at all costs. We'll talk in much more detail about this in chapter three. For now, just know that debt is an enemy of time, and put simply is just your current-self stealing from your future-self.

Just because you're down on luck today, doesn't mean you have to be tomorrow, or a year from now.

Time is Forever Changing

Some people have had bad stuff happen to them and wanted to give up. However, if you think back to those events now, years later, you realize your life continued to march on. Maybe you had a car repossessed, you became disabled, or you lost a job or loved one; life just really put you to the test. It's times like these your emotional intelligence and control is put to the test. From a time perspective you'll have to remember a year or two from now things will be OK, life will go on, and that the world is forever changing. If you're managing your time correctly and you have realistic objectives you'll accomplish your goals while in the driver seat, climbing up the skyscraper of life.

A Schedule is the Key

Purpose

Thus far in this chapter we've discussed how time is short and finite. Not only shouldn't you waste it, but you have to think of it from a high-level and as a whole. We talked about the importance of a work/life balance, and discussed a few drugs – or toxic activities – to time. We expressed how time management at its core is the administration of your time. And you should plan your time strategically instead of leaving it to chance. I'd like to quickly dissect each of these five pieces as they relate to a schedule to show why and when a schedule is necessary to anyone who has goals.

1. **Time is Short and Finite, View it as a Whole at a High-Level** – This concept is a canvas for a schedule. From a schedule's perspective you must understand your goals to break them down into smaller pieces. Remember in chapter one we discussed breaking the elephant into smaller pieces to more easily tackle an issue, as opposed to trying to tackle the big issue all at once. If your goal is to become a professor teaching bachelor level students, then there are many milestones you'll have to accomplish. A schedule must view your life as a whole at a high-level. This allows the ability to tie key milestones in life to specific ages. For example, if you want to be this professor by age 30, then you'll need to start grad school to get your master's degree by age 27, which means you'll need a bachelor's degree before then. That helps you understand when you'll need to accomplish specific objectives to reach a goal. This concept was presented because it's the reason schedules are needed.
2. **Work/Life Balance** – When we work a job we're typically provided with a schedule, whether it's consistent or not. However, many of us in our personal life have no schedule we follow consistently. Because of this we can't measure or manage our non-work time well. For workaholics, this may mean you neglect home life because you're consistently working. For others, it means you waste a lot of your free time not accomplishing many

objectives towards goals and dreams. This concept was brought up because it points out any organized body such as the military or a business uses schedules to accomplish their objectives. Waking up to this fact and incorporating a schedule in your personal life to accomplish your goals is the point of this concept.

3. **Drugs to Time** – Some people spend a lot of time on social media apps. The majority of these individuals don't have a schedule in their personal lives. When you make the transition from not managing/scheduling your personal time to someone who follows a personal calendar, you will be tempted by the drugs of time (i.e., social media, reality TV, unproductive tasks). Remember, that you have a schedule and stick to it just like you do your work schedule! The purpose of this concept was to warn you that drugs to time will try to distract you from your schedule, slowing you or preventing you from accomplishing your goals.

4. **Time Administration** – A schedule removes time administration decisions from your emotions, and allows you to strategically manage and take control of your time. Remember, time administration is simply deciding what you do with your time. With a schedule you're in control while in the driver seat.

5. **Strategically Planning Time** – This concept was introduced because it is the compass of a schedule. This should be done daily at first. Once you've traveled high enough in the skyscraper of life, you'll have enough experience to only update your schedule once a week.

"Implementing a schedule allows *you* to decide how you spend *your* time!"

When to Use a Schedule

We talked about why a schedule is needed, and key aspects around a schedule. However, we haven't covered when a schedule is needed. Some of you may be thinking this guy takes all the fun and impulsiveness out of life. You would be entirely wrong. A schedule is not meant to control 100% of your life. A schedule is only needed for the important tasks in your life that are required to help you achieve your goals. So, the example earlier around if you wanted to become a professor, the objectives you must achieve for that goal, those must be scheduled. If you want to get in shape or stay in shape, working out must be scheduled. If there are tasks you must complete to achieve a goal, then those tasks should be scheduled. Again, the reason we discuss the work/life balance is because you need to understand the more aggressive your goals, the more of your life you'll need to schedule. Meaning, if you're the type of person who doesn't like a structured life, then don't set aggressive goals! Regardless of your goals or how much of your life you schedule, it's imperative you have specific items on your schedule.

How do you spend your time, specifically?

Contents of a Schedule

When your mind is first opened to the fact that organized establishments utilize schedules to accomplish objectives, and that when used in your personal life you can easily accomplish the same, the next question is what do you put into a schedule. There are short-term schedules, typically done on a weekly basis, and there are long-term schedules. Before you can create a short-term schedule, such as a weekly schedule, you must create a long-term schedule; so, let's start there. As we start our long-term schedule we know some of our objectives as we laid them out in the actions section of chapter one, right? However, without a structure your personal long-term schedule will not be as effective or efficient. I recommend you have five areas on your schedule: education, physical personal growth, mental personal growth, career, and standard of life. Below is a screenshot from an Excel spreadsheet demonstrating many of the sections I'm referring to. You'll notice each column is a quarter – which consists of 3 months. For example, Q1 18 – or quarter one 2018 – consists of the months January, February, and March. If you're not good with Excel, maybe use tables in a word document, or even a notebook (pen and paper). Below we'll talk through in detail what should go into each section and when to use a specific area.

	Q1 18	Q2 18	Q3 18	Q4 18	Q1 19
EDUCATION					
PERSONAL GROWTH					
Physical					
Mental					
CAREER					

- **Education** – We covered education in chapter one briefly. Suffice it to say, if you're on a path that requires education you put your quarterly goals in this section. If you've completed college, what certifications can you acquire to make more money? Now if a certificate isn't applicable and you've acquired the degrees needed for your path, then it's OK for this section to be blank.
- **Physical Personal Growth** – In chapter six we'll talk about health in more detail. However, this is the section in your schedule where you list your physical goals. Maybe you're looking to lose some weight, or looking to tone up. Any physical goal, even walking a specific number of steps, is what goes in this section of your schedule.
- **Mental Personal Growth** – This is a section I typically refer to as lifelong learning. For example, do you know how a car loan, home mortgage, the banking system in your country, or taxes work? These are all things that will affect most of you, yet few of you could answer, "Yes I understand all those topics in detail." The point is outside of structured official education you must continue to learn if you wish to climb the skyscraper of life. Create a list of ten things you wish you knew about, and then put them on your schedule accordingly.
- **Career** – This section may not be as self-explanatory as most think. It requires a lot of research to populate this section accurately. The screenshot provided above only shows quarters for this year and next. However, your long-term schedule should show five years broken out as follows: the previous year, the current year, and three years into the future. Now some of you are thinking, "how will I know where I'll be in my career in three years?" You already know the answer; you're in the driver seat so you'll be wherever you've planned to be. For example, if you're an analyst and want to become a senior analyst, you must research the education, skills, and experience that is required to apply for a senior analyst position. Then you schedule out the applicable actions to obtain the education, skills, and experience needed. Doing so will tell you when you'll apply and acquire that position. We'll break this down in much more detail to answer many questions in chapter six. For now, simply know this section of your long-term schedule is for placing your career objectives.

Steady Growth

Your Current Self

In the previous section we discussed a long-term schedule stretching across five years to track the various objectives you must accomplish to get to where you want to go in life. That schedule is imperative, but it's only a roadmap to refer to once a quarter to ensure you're on the right track and make course adjustments as needed. It's a visual representation of the path, or road, you're currently on. Until you take the time to create one it's difficult to see if you've accomplished the right tasks in the past 12 months. Some choose to do a vision board, but that method doesn't allow for easy tracking of objectives. This long-term schedule not only puts your current path into perspective because it's visual, but it outlines how you can adjust course onto either a new, better path, or onto the next path in your journey.

Once you've drafted a long-term schedule you're now ready to begin your short-term schedule. The purpose of a short-term schedule is to manage your weekly time to ensure during the thirteen weeks in the quarter you accomplish the objectives for that quarter - as outlined on your long-term schedule. Now notice how I worded that. When you look at your goals & objectives from the perspective of time, you have only thirteen weeks, it shifts your paradigm. This helps you start to figure out what needs to be done each week of those thirteen weeks if you want to finish that goal on time. In chapter six we'll show you how to do this in detail. For now, know this assigning of tasks to weeks and ensuring most days of the week you work on your tasks, that is time management.

"You typically must grow to accomplish life goals worth attaining."

Your Future Self

I know many of these concepts are not new to some of you. But do you practice all of these today? Most of you will answer no. What you're not getting is that these are all parts needed to get you moving up the skyscraper quickly. Sure, you'll move up the skyscraper one step at a time. However, if you want your dreams and goals quicker why not be more efficient? For most of you the answer is simple, you don't know how. I honestly think it's ridiculous everyone isn't taught how to manage time better in high school. Remember, nobody owes you anything. If you want it, go get it! Your future self will love you for it.

Are you where you thought you would be at your age?

Your Past Paths

Now one important point I want to cover before we leave the schedule area is a major misconception many individuals have around changing their lives. Some people with a lot of debt, or bad pasts feel it's not possible for them to have a happily ever after future. You're absolutely wrong. Until you believe me on this, you'll keep on the same path feeling like you don't have a choice – the "ignorance is bliss" bug. You should know by now, you're in the driver seat, you decide. I bring this up because I want everyone to realize that once you start up the skyscraper of life, the previous paths will become less relevant. For those of you with a college degree, it's much like getting your first college degree; your high school diploma or GED no longer maters. Once you have a college degree no one will ask or care about your high school diploma. When you learn to build and follow a schedule, you've opened the doors to success. Instead of wasting time listing all the reasons you can't do it, why don't you just make a schedule and do it!?

Dangerous Paths

The Dangerous Path

I've had some people tell me, "A schedule is simply a list of tasks I need to do." And they are correct. The difference though is a schedule allows you to view that list from a time perspective and force prioritizes everything on the list. The last part is the key part, a force prioritized list. That means everything is sorted from the most important to the least important. So, if you can only accomplish five items you knock out the five most important items. Basically, a schedule provides an external tool to help your brain do what it needs in order to get things done. However, a schedule can be harmful and lead you down a dangerous path. Obviously having no schedule means you're moving slowly up the skyscraper of life, and you will either take some time to reach your destination or just not accomplish as much in your life. On the flip side, if you have a schedule that is overwhelming or fails to help you prioritize what is really important then the schedule can be harmful.

Are you on a dangerous path, or know someone who is?

Outcomes

So how do you ensure you're not on a dangerous path? There are two parts to figuring this out: first, ensuring you have the right items planned out strategically, which we'll cover in detail in chapter six. The second part is to manage your schedule closely to ensure you catch any issues quickly before they turn into a dangerous path. To do this, simply plan your day the night before if possible. In situations where this isn't possible, then plan early in the day. This allows you to look over the schedule regularly to ensure you're accomplishing the right tasks every day. This also makes it easier to course correct as well. In short, it gives you the outcomes you want. If you didn't accomplish a task you scheduled for that day, don't fret. Simply move it to the next day when you plan out your next day. Now if this happens a second time, it's time for you to do a self-analysis asking yourself two questions:

1. Why have I not accomplished the same task twice now?
2. What do I need to change to ensure this does not occur again?

If you don't have the knowledge to answer these questions yourself, ask close friends, family members, or a mentor; but you absolutely must answer the questions! It's *this* process that ensures your schedule stays healthy. When something derails your schedule, you must delineate between controllable and uncontrollable items. For uncontrollable items you pick yourself back up, and get back on the path, life goes on. For controllable items they are like a common cold to your schedule. Once they happen three or four times they become the flu – and you don't want your schedule to die. That's why this is the third of the ten well-guarded secrets about life, **you must protect your schedule's health as if it were your own, because it is your planned future's health.**

"Unmanaged dangerous paths can have tragic endings - if traveled for too long."

You Are a Sum of Who You Surround Yourself With

Now that you've learned the first three well-guarded secret about life, let's talk about a major risk to all of them. Remember the first well-guarded secret is that you must learn emotional intelligence, or emotions may sabotage your success. You also learned you're in the driver seat, responsible and accountable for taking yourself wherever you're willing to go. Although more people are starting to learn this concept, not many fully get it. And the third was you must protect your schedule's health as if it were your own, because it is your planned future's health. There's a tad bit of wisdom I must share with you for you to understand this major risk to all the secrets learned thus far. That is, due largely in part to the law of attraction, you are a sum of the top five to six individuals you surround yourself with. As it relates to your schedule, this means if you find the main reason your schedule's cold is becoming a flu is because a friend or person who is around you a lot, you must cut those ties. Or at least minimize interaction. I know how cold-hearted this sounds. However, I made it very clear you can get to where ever you want to go, if you're willing to do what it takes to get there. If a specific person in your life continually derails your objectives/schedule, then either you must discuss how that can stop, or they've got to go! If you're not willing to do this then your schedule will continually be interrupted, with your goals taking longer and longer to obtain – and that's if you reach them at all. Most individuals learn this lesson the hard way at some point in their life. Until you accept this you may have trouble reaching your destination in the skyscraper.

Opportunities – Don't Miss Your Shot!

Before but Especially After College

Even following a schedule perfectly, what will differentiate you from everyone else smart enough to research, schedule, and meet objectives? How do you stand out in the crowd? You've learned a schedule and managing your time are keys to success in the skyscraper of life, each one an opportunity for you to get to where you want to be much faster. However, you also have to keep an eye out for opportunities! This skill is what will differentiate you from the crowd. If there's something that seems out of the norm, ask yourself how this can be an opportunity? Some opportunities may require you to leave much of your current life behind. Other opportunities may require you to learn new things quickly, or change what you do on a daily basis. Some will take you backwards and slow you down. The important thing is that you learn how to identify an opportunity and don't be afraid to take a chance. You see friends taking great vacations, exploring the world, buying nice homes, cars, living great lives. You may ask yourself, "what are they doing that I'm not?" "Why am I still struggling living pay check to paycheck?" It's simple; they found an opportunity and took it! It's not enough just to follow the schedule and accomplish goals; you must identify and take opportunities, and quickly before others do.

"There's an opportunity around every corner."

Maximizing Time

I hope by this point you'll know the answer to this question: how can you maximize the amount of time you have available in life, to accomplish all you'd like to accomplish? That's right, have a schedule, follow a schedule, and manage any risks to the schedule – keep it healthy. Until you learn time management well it will be difficult to maximize your time towards your dreams. Review the chapter two summary thoroughly and ensure you feel comfortable with all the concepts of this chapter. After the summary if you think you get it, and understand the importance of time management, then you're in a great spot. After reading the summary continue on to the chapter two actions section to continue building out the system you'll use to get you to where you want to be in the skyscraper of life.

Chapter Two Summary - Time, a Rare Resource

Background to Time

In this chapter you learned that you must track your time closely as it's finite; you learned how you spend your time determines how much you'll get out of life. So, it's important you utilize time management in order to get what you want, time has no take backs. Life is literally what you make of it. As we live such a short life span we must view life from a high-level to thoroughly plan for all of it, including retirement. It's imperative you know your life goals and personal drive to determine a good work/life balance. And be keenly aware that there are a few drugs to time you must watch out for and manage if you want your schedule to be successful.

Long-Term & Short-Term Schedules

You learned that time management, when in the context of your life, is really time administration. You should decide what you do with your time, not leave it up to your emotions and chance. Financial debt is locked doors in the skyscraper of life, slowing you down on getting you to where you want to go. But time is forever changing and you can always choose a different path – you're in the driver seat! Using a schedule allows you to control *your* time to get you to where you want. However, schedules are not always needed. Schedules, although helpful in many situations, are really only essential for any objectives in your life required to achieve your goals. And for a long-term quarter-by-quarter schedule to cover all the important areas of your life, it should have five key areas: education, physical personal growth, mental personal growth, career, and standard of living. This schedule will help guide you, one objective at a time, to your goals in life. However, you must utilize a short-term schedule to manage the 13 weeks in a quarter such that you successfully achieve each objective. Ultimately, schedules help you easily navigate the skyscraper of life.

Past and Dangerous Paths

The past is the past, leave it there and always look to the future. Once you reach a new phase, previous phases matter less and less. But don't follow a schedule blindly as some lead to a dangerous path. If you have a schedule that is overwhelming or fails to help you prioritize what is really important, then the schedule can be harmful. Although you may not have known all of this material I hope you realize there's a reason why every organized group uses schedules to get things done, because they work. Once you've graduated to using schedules, you have to manage your schedule closely to ensure you catch any issues quickly before they turn into a dangerous path. There may be controllable aspects about your life that are like a common cold to your schedule. Once they happen three or four times they become the flu – and you don't want your schedule to die. That's why the third of the ten well-guarded secrets about life is that **you must protect your schedule's health as if it were your own, because it is your planned future's health.** You are a sum of who you surround yourself with; so surround yourself with people who support your schedule's health – like a gym partner, study buddy, a mentor, or friends that make you happy in your down time that supports your goals.

Chapter Two Action – Planned Schedule

In chapter one we started building a system to get you to where you want to go. This system, when complete, will have multiple parts. As you grow with each chapter, you'll not only build out new sections, you'll also gain new responsibilities to support this system. The good news about chapter two's action is that you do not have to complete it before moving further through the book. For now, simply fill in what you know, and we'll come back to the rest later. However, do not move to chapter three until you've completed at least populating what you know.

In chapter one you created a very high-level long-term schedule with three data points (i.e., current year, three years from now, and six years from now). A true long-term schedule requires measurable objectives, typically by quarter. Plus, recall what you learned earlier. Your long-term schedule should show five years broken out as follows: the previous year, the current year, and each of the next three years into the future. As our objectives are quarterly, our long-term schedule must show each of our five years by quarters. On the next page you'll find the graph you should create using Excel or pen and paper. This chart will be the first piece to your new system that will allow you to get to where you want to go in life. Once created, fill out what you know. You'll complete all other areas you may not know in chapter six, when you'll also create your short-term schedule. You'll find an example of a fully populated long-term schedule on the page after the provided template.

For anyone thinking of skipping this action, you'll be going against the fourth most well-guarded secret about life; **following through is critical to success, especially when creating and following your system.** You will absolutely not be successful if you can't step up and follow through.

Chapter Two Template

Year & Age	Year	Education	Career	Personal Growth	Physical Growth	Standard of Living
2018 23y/o Previous Year	Quarter 1					
	Quarter 2					
	Quarter 3					
	Quarter 4					
2019 24y/o Current Year	Quarter 1					
	Quarter 2					
	Quarter 3					
	Quarter 4					
2020 25y/o	Quarter 1					
	Quarter 2					
	Quarter 3					
	Quarter 4					
2021 26y/o	Quarter 1					
	Quarter 2					
	Quarter 3					
	Quarter 4					
2022 27y/o	Quarter 1					
	Quarter 2					
	Quarter 3					
	Quarter 4					
2025 30y/o Distant Future	2025					

Chapter Two Example

Year & Age	Year	Education	Career	Personal Growth	Physical Growth	Standard of Living
2018 23 Previous Year	Quarter 1	Work on Associates 16 Credit Hrs.	Server Experience		Gain 5 pounds	2015 Corolla 3 BR Apt Expenses = $200 a wk. 3 Vacations a Year
	Quarter 2					
	Quarter 3					
	Quarter 4					
2019 24 Current Year	Quarter 1	Work on Associates 24 Credit Hrs.	Server Experience	Obtain CervSafe Certifications	Workout Consistently	2015 Toyota Corolla 3 BR Apt Expenses = $250 a wk. 3 Vacations a Year
	Quarter 2				Run a 5K	
	Quarter 3			Obtain CPR Certifications	Workout	
	Quarter 4				Gain 5 pounds	
2020 25	Quarter 1	Complete Associates 24 Credit Hrs.	Start at a hotel for hotel experience	Join Lodging Association	Gain 5 pounds	2018 Honda Accord Luxury 3 BR Apt. Expenses = $250 a wk. 4 Vacations a Year
	Quarter 2				Run a 5K	
	Quarter 3			Start Learning Spanish	Tone up Body	
	Quarter 4				Workout	
2021 26	Quarter 1	Work on Bachelors 30 Credit Hrs.		Learn all areas of a hotel and Spanish	Tone up Body	2018 Honda Accord Luxury 3 BR Apt. Expenses = $300 a wk. 4 Vacations a Year
	Quarter 2				Run a 5K	
	Quarter 3				Workout	
	Quarter 4				Run a 5K	
2022 27	Quarter 1	Complete Bachelors 30 Credit Hrs.	Get into hotel mgmt.	Learn all areas of a hotel and Spanish	Workout	2018 Honda Accord Luxury 3 BR Apt. Expenses = $350 a wk. 4 Vacations a Year
	Quarter 2				Run a 5K	
	Quarter 3				Workout	
	Quarter 4				Run a 5K	
2025 30 Distant Future	2025	Obtain Masters	Front Desk Mgr.	Obtain Hotel Industry Certification	Run two 5Ks	2023 Lexus New 4 BR House

Chapter 3
Money, a Rare Resource

"The way to get started is to quit talking and start doing."

- Walt Disney

Introduction

At this point you've learned four of the ten well-guarded secrets about life. For those of you confused by me saying four, and are thinking we only covered three, then you really do not understand the purpose of this book and should stop reading to save yourself time – because this is one of the hardest chapters with three sections to its actions. So why am I saying this? Because if you performed the actions in Chapter 2, actually took action to get experience, you would have learned the fourth most well-guarded secret about life. This book is a tool, meant to help you build your system, the system to get you to where you want to be. If you refuse to take the actions needed to get you there, then why read about how to do it? If you did not start your chapter two actions, please do so before proceeding. The skyscraper of life is a large complex place; complete your actions to build out your system to navigate successfully to where you're trying to go.

For those of you who have taken the time to start your chapter two actions, great! You should now have a long-term schedule either partially or fully populated. So, at this point you've learned you have to capitalize on opportunities. Unfortunately, some of these opportunities cost money. Most of us are barely treading water financially. There's really no money for opportunities. How can you change that? The answer is the same solution as with managing your time, build a system. For time, schedules are the systems used. For money, a budget is needed. But before we get into the details of a budget it's important to understand the objectives of a budget.

Why do you budget?

Your Plan Must be Funded

You're aware of the "ignorance is bliss" bug, so you know there are many things we just don't know about life. One of these things is, it typically costs money to get to where you want to be, and that's one objective of the budget. Just as a schedule manages your time to achieve goals, a budget manages your money to ensure you can financially survive while funding your schedule. Many feel the two are separate entities, but the truth is they are interconnected. One will fail without the other. We first taught you emotional intelligence skills are required to ensure your emotions don't sabotage your goals. You also learned you're in the driver seat; you can go wherever you're willing to go. Then we taught you not only are schedules needed, but they also must be protected as if it were your own health, because it is your planned future's health. Finally, we covered the hardest of all the secrets to master, following through with your system. In this chapter we're going to cover how you'll fund your trip through the skyscraper, so you can achieve all your dreams.

Do you truthfully budget?

Areas of a Budget

In order to understand why each section should go on your budget, it's important to remember the two objectives of a budget. First, a good budget should be designed in such a way that it continually maintains or increases your credit score. In chapter four we'll get into complete detail around how your credit score is calculated, and how to manage each area within your budget to ensure your credit score is where you want it to be. And as mentioned before, the second purpose of a budget is to fund your schedule so you can get to where you want to in the skyscraper of life. Understanding the two objectives of a budget will help you understand why there are key pieces on the budget.

As you progress through your life phases you'll have new areas appear on your budget. For example, if your goal is to buy a house or other assets, you'll need an area on your budget to manage that. As this book is not geared for individuals successful enough to have multiple assets, we'll be covering just the basics I feel everyone should have at minimum on their budget. Each of the items fall into one of three buckets, either daily tasks, weekly tasks, or monthly tasks. In the monthly tasks you have the debt, credit card, and forecast management sections of the budget. For daily and weekly tasks, you have tracking your income, costs, and spending. In the next few sections we'll cover each section in detail so that you can create your own later. In addition to these areas of a budget there's also a Funds and Plan section we'll talk about later in this chapter.

Monthly tasks you should have are debt, credit card, and forecast management.

Monthly Tasks – Debt

As mentioned previously the areas of the budget that fall into monthly budget tasks are the Debt Management, Credit Card Management, and Forecast Management sections of your budget. In the next few sections of this chapter we'll do a deep dive into each section and explain what should be within it. We'll talk about how some debt is needed, but only good debt. We'll talk about how you should be making money from your credit cards if you're using them correctly – and teach you how to do this. And then we'll talk through what a forecast is, why it's needed and the various sections of a forecast.

"Everyone should have some debt, but good debt."

Debt

Most people know what debt is. However, just to level set, debt is something, typically money, goods or services, that is due or owed. Many people who have debt they can't afford to pay off defaults to the "ignorance is bliss" bug state and ignores the debt. The thought process is, "I'm barely making it, I can't afford this debt!" However, this is simply tearing your credit score up. Remember, one of the budget's objectives is to ensure your credit score isn't decreasing. This Debt section of your budget should list all of your debts, good and bad. However, when listing your debt, it's best to group it by good debt or bad debt. For each item of debt, you should list the following: Debt name, Debt Amount, and if you're making monthly payments, the Debt Monthly Due Dates and Monthly Payment Amount. Now don't worry about memorizing all of this. We'll create your Debt section of your budget in the actions section of this chapter.

Types of Debt

When creditors look at your credit, specifically your debt, not all debt is equal. Meaning, some debt creditors understand is part of life and they don't count it against you. Now depending on the creditor this changes. However, a good rule of thumb to follow is if the debt is supporting a future investment such as student loans or a mortgage, then creditors will typically see that as good debt - and these types of debt will help your credit score, especially the more diversified you have your debt. However, if you have debt collectors trying to collect money, or credit card debt, these types of debt are seen as bad debt by creditors, mainly because it shows poor judgement in managing your credit.

Ignoring Debt

Now as some of you begin writing down your debt, you're going to get concerned about how much negative debt you have – and stressed about how you're going to take care of it. STOP THAT! You will never get past this obstacle in the skyscraper of life if you can't control your emotions. This type of stressful emotion leads to people ignoring debt. Now as you know, you're in the driver seat. So, take charge of your life and be aware of your financial environment, specifically where you stand with your debt. Doing so will allow you to solve how to get rid of this risk.

How are you managing your debt?

Get Advice

Having your debt written down allows you to look at it as it relates to the rest of your budget, to determine how you'll get rid of the debt. If you're not well versed in how to best get out of debt, I recommend a financial advisor if you're in a pretty tough spot, or for tighter budgets try a life coach. A therapist helps you with past issues. In contrasts, a life coach ignores your past and simply helps you get to where you want to be in the future. There are many different life coaches with varying costs. One good company is The Real Consultants. Feel free to check out their information in the back of the book in the section entitled recommendations by the author. At the end of the day, you should have a section in your budget named "Debt," that's listing all of your debt and is updated on a monthly basis.

Monthly Tasks - Credit Cards

The next monthly task we're discussing is credit card management. Now many people have had their lives majorly affected in a negative way by credit cards, and there's an equal amount of people who truthfully have no idea how credit cards work.

Despite what you've heard, there are two important things you should know about credit cards. First, everyone should have multiple credit cards. Secondly, you should get a credit card as early in your life as possible. Now those of you who were told the opposite, were unfortunately told this by someone who doesn't know how to use credit cards – or they may have very little faith that you'll be able to use a credit card correctly. For the individuals who fall in the latter (i.e., someone having very little faith that you'll be able to use a credit card correctly), I dare you to prove them wrong – you're in the driver seat!

Rewards

So why is it so important you have multiple credit cards? One reason is because when used correctly credit cards should be a source of income. That's right, when used correctly you make money from your credit cards. Certain credit cards have something called credit card rewards. Although they vary, most typically they allow you to trade your rewards in for gift cards or credit to your account. I typically fund most of my black Friday or Christmas shopping from my credit card rewards. If you're looking to get your first or second credit card, you may not be able to get a credit card with rewards. The rule of thumb around getting a credit card is to ensure there's no annual fee, don't get more than two or three new cards in a six to twelve-month window, and ensure the credit card has rewards.

Are you making money from your credit cards?

Using Credit Cards

So how do you correctly use a credit card to make money? It's simple; ensure credit cards are never a cost. To do this you must do two things. First, ensure you have no minimum payments to pay. Secondly, ensure you have no interest charges. You can accomplish both by paying off anything you put on credit cards within 30 days. Sometimes credit cards have deals where there's no interest for a short period. This can also be helpful for minimizing cost or moving debt to lower costs. The point of this section is to ensure you know that as long as you use credit cards when you know you'll have the money to pay it off in the next 30 days, then you'll - in time - begin making money from your credit cards. We'll get into this topic in a lot more detail in the next chapter when we talk about your credit score.

Downfalls of Using Credit

There are many downsides to credit cards when they're not used correctly. This is why credit cards fall into the monthly tasks bucket. At the end of each month you should update and review the credit card section of your budget. In this section you should have the following information for each credit card: Credit card name, its monthly due date, its current minimum payment, the credit limit, the current balance, and how much you paid in interest for that month. Just like with the debt information, the details in this section will be used to get you to where you want to go. If ever a credit card is higher than expected, you'll need to understand why, correct what caused it to be too high, and plan accordingly.

Everyone should utilize credit cards!

Monthly Tasks - Forecast

The final of the three budgeting areas that fall into monthly tasks is Forecast Management. A forecast is an estimate, or prediction, of the future in some way. As it relates to your budget, the forecast looks at the coming months to determine all income and costs. However, when designed properly your forecast should divide all your costs in a meaningful way. The budgeting system we're going to use in this chapter's action area to create your forecast is the 50/30/20 method.

"The way you spend your money today, affects the way you live tomorrow."

50/30/20 Budgeting Method

As stated previously, it's important to divide all your costs in a meaningful way. The reason is so you know how your financial allocation compares to the amount of money you should ideally spend on various items. The 50/30/20 method is a simple and widely used way to bucket your costs. First, you must calculate your after-tax income. After-tax income is the amount of money you make after taxes are taken out of your check (e.g., state tax, federal tax, Medicare and Social Security tax). If retirement, health care, or any other deductions are taken from your check, be sure to add them back in. Determine how many checks you receive this month and calculate your monthly income. If you work in an industry with tips, you simply add all your cash received with your after-tax income from your checks. The goal of this section is to walk you through how to calculate your after-tax monthly income. With this number you're ready to divide it up into three chunks, 50%, 30%, and 20% (e.g., If your after tax monthly income is $2,000, it would be split 50%-$1,000, 30%-$600, and 20%-$400).

50% - Essential Costs

Once you know your monthly income, you need to list out all your costs per month. Once you feel you've listed all your monthly costs, note how much you spend on any needed item such as rent, utilities, insurance, healthcare, groceries, etc... The essential costs or needed items should never be more than 50% of your total after-tax income for the month. Now, many of you will probably struggle with what is a "need" and what is a "want." For example, some of you would bucket your cable bill or your back-to-school clothing into this 50% bucket as a "need," and that would be incorrect. The rule of thumb is if you can miss a payment with little punishment, then it's not needed. On the flip side, if missing a payment would severely impact your quality of life, such as missing your rent, then it's a need. One area that is always confusing is credit card minimum payments. These are to be added in this section under "need" as paying the minimum balance is required on credit cards to not harm your credit score.

30% - Lifestyle Choices

Once all your needs and essential costs are marked accordingly on your list of costs, you're ready for your wants. Go back to your list of monthly costs and add up the costs for all the "wants." These should not exceed 30% of your after-tax monthly income. Many feel that 30% of their income spent on their wants is pretty high. However, these are also the same people who have many "wants" in their "needs" bucket. For example, shopping for anything not essential for work or bare minimums is a want. Dollar Shave Club, cable TV, vacations, restaurants, unlimited text messaging plan, etc... Most people who don't track their costs closely spend much more on "wants" than they think.

Are you spending your money right?

20% - Savings & Debt

20% of your after-tax income should be spent on saving money for a rainy day, retirement and repaying debts. If you have any credit card debt the minimum payment is a "need" as expressed previously – counting towards the 50% essential costs bucket. Any payment to the credit card greater than the minimum payment is an additional debt repayment, which means it should fall within this 20% section. If you have a car loan, the premise is the same. The minimum car loan payment is a "need," and anything extra paid falls into this bucket, the 20%.

Debt, credit cards, and forecasts are three sections that your budget should have, and should be reviewed thoroughly on a monthly basis. This is critical in managing your credit score and future plans! Reviewing thoroughly monthly will ensure you manage each in the direction needed to get you to where you want to go in the skyscraper of life.

Daily & Weekly Budget Tasks

In the previous sections we discussed the three tasks you should perform on your budget monthly: One is debt; you should review *all* of your debt monthly; second is credit cards, you should review and know the minimum payment, current balance, and any interest paid, for each credit card owned monthly; And finally, you should review your forecast, fully understanding all income and costs you'll incur for the current and next few months in the important 50/30/20 buckets.

Now let's take a look into the daily and weekly tasks: tracking your income, costs, and spending. With the forecast you know where all of your monthly income should be spent. The daily and weekly tasks allow you to track your activity to ensure your actual actions align with your planned ones. This is critical for the big picture to work. First, we're going to review the two areas of the budget that should be reviewed on nearly a daily basis, the section where you track your income and costs.

Many things are possible with a budget!

Managing Income and Costs

There's many ways to track your income and costs. I personally use an Excel spreadsheet. Let's first tackle income, most businesses allow your checks to be direct deposited. If that's not an option, be sure to deposit your check and not cash it. This allows you to quickly and easily see in your bank statement – preferably online – how much you made and on what day. In your budget you keep track of when you got paid and how much money you made, remember only after-tax income. For those of you who receive tips, your income is cash nearly daily. Same actions apply though, simply track how much you made, and which day you made the money. Then the most important step, deposit your cash; do NOT spend any cash unless you absolutely have to. By using only credit cards for all purchases it makes it really easy to track spending and costs for any expenditures. This is important so you don't have to spend much time managing your budget.

So, we just covered income, pretty much deposit checks and most importantly don't spend cash, only use credit cards. Now let's switch gears to talk about costs. I have two important things to cover on this topic. First, setup every bill or reoccurring monthly payment on auto-pay – get this done before the end of this month. Set everything up on only those credit cards that receive rewards. If you don't have any credit cards that offer rewards, any credit card will do – but work to get a credit card that receives rewards ASAP! I understand some bills will only allow payment through a bank account for auto-pay, or they may charge a fee for paying with credit. In these scenarios simply utilize your bank account to set up the auto-payment. If you don't have a checking account, research and get a free checking account this week – I'm serious, grab a pen and paper and take note to get this done if you fall into this bucket!

Managing Your Income

Managing your budget as described above has many benefits. Immediately depositing your checks or cash ensures that all income made is immediately put into a bank account to cover any upcoming auto-payments. Choosing to set up all costs on credit cards and on auto payment ensures you never are late on a bill - which significantly affects your credit score. It also means that you can easily track all your costs and verify that everything you anticipated to be paid got paid, and for the amount expected. A budget is nothing more than a means to structure all this information so that you can easily track that you are where you want to be. A budget is the tool to manage your income. It's meant to protect the important areas of your life such as your credit score, critical monthly bills, and future endeavors; while also being that annoying reminder that you have rules to follow – you can't just go out and do whatever you want financially. However, when the rules are followed you get exactly what you put in your budget, accomplishing your goals one objective at a time.

More Money Each Year

Why Make More?

Once you have a budget in place and you're managing your income and cost, the next objective is to make more money. Asking someone why this would be the next objective will get you many interesting responses. Many individuals will be inaccurate in their responses. Some will talk about what they want to purchase, others what their desires are. Truth though, from a budget perspective you want to make more money so that you can put more income into funds and the plan. However, before we dive into those topics let's talk about how you can make more money year-over-year.

How to Make More?

There are many ways to make more money. Many of the activities you have in your schedule to improve yourself and grow will help you get to positions in your career where you will have more money. However, some years you could use a little help. One easy way to make more money is to look for promotions to open new checking accounts. Many banks will run promotions offering a free amount of money by simply opening a checking account with their bank. Taking advantage of three to six of these offers per year allows for a nice boost in income. You can always pick up a part-time job serving, or delivering papers. If you struggle with finding ways to make more money I recommend you reach out to a Life Coach. A Life Coach can help you identify opportunities that may help you make more money.

Did you make more money last year than you did the previous year?

More in Funds and Plan!

In the previous section we talked about making more money year-over-year so you can put more money in funds and the plan. When thinking about the budget at a high-level you have your income that you bring in, and you have your fixed set of bills. Once all your costs are paid for, you typically have some money left over. This left over money should go in one of three locations. First, your expenses, the money you're allowed to spend on a daily basis for living expenses such as food or entertainment. The second bucket is funds. And for you smart ones, the third bucket is the plan. So, let's talk about what these buckets of funds and the plan really are.

Funds

Mitigate Risks

Have you ever had anybody ask you for gas money? Or have you heard anyone say, "every time things go right something always goes wrong." These individuals have something in common; they don't manage their short- term risks. A fund is when you take a subset of money and set it to the side to use for a particular purpose. You set up funds so you don't have to worry about short-term risks. For example, you may have a gas fund. If you owe deductibles for your medical benefits, you may have a medical fund. If you have pets, they require supplies, food, maintenance; you should have a pet fund.

By figuring out how much money you need per month for a particular fund your able to set aside that money upfront to ensure you have nothing to worry about around that particular topic. Of course, until you get to the point in the skyscraper of life where you're making more money year-over-year, it will be difficult to have enough extra income to put into multiple funds.

Funds manage your short-term risks in life.

Pay for the mitigations

Many of you have money for funds today. If you recall the previous section of this chapter covering the forecast of your budget, there are three areas that all your costs fall into: Lifestyle Choices, Essential Expenses, and Financial Priorities. Funds go under lifestyle choices. At the end of this chapter, we're going to make the forecast for your life. Once you create your forecast, go back and look at your lifestyle choices to see if yours is 30% of your income. You're going to find one of two scenarios. The first is those of you who spend way too much in Lifestyle Choices. However, instead of spending the money on important items like funds, much of it is spent on items you want – but don't absolutely need. The second group is those who spend much less than 30% in Lifestyle Choices. These individuals are typically spending much more in essential expenses, or they have a lot of debt they're paying off. However, if and when you're spending 30% of your income on Lifestyle Choices as you should, you typically have money to put into funds. For those who complain that bad stuff always happens, how do you ensure you don't have to worry about the little things? It's simple, when setting up your forecast ensure that you put some of your income into funds. Leaving it at zero is the same as saying you're inviting the short-term risk to come interrupt your life.

How do you ensure you don't have to worry about the little things?

Less Worry in Life

Remember, not everything in life is controllable. There will be risks that come up that are entirely out of your control. However, many situations we're presented are in our control. As you learned in chapter 1, you're in the driver seat. Once you realize the importance of funds and start utilizing them in your forecast, you'll spend less time worrying about controllable things and more time accomplishing your life goals. For items out of your control all you can do is simply analyze your situation and get back on your path. For everything else, from a short-term monthly basis, there're funds.

The Plan

Putting it on The Plan

In the previous section we talked about funds and the importance of having these in place to manage your short-term risks in life. Once you have all your costs covered, including your short-term risks, you're now ready to put money in the plan. The plan is how you get things done. For most of us to get to where we're trying to get in the skyscraper of life it will cost us money. Unless you have wealthy family members willing to give you money to get there, you have to put the money aside monthly in the plan to ensure you get to where you want to be. Just like funds, the plan goes in the Lifestyle Choices section of the forecast. So again, for those of you looking at your forecast and not putting 30% in Lifestyle Choices, you're not managing the short-term risks in your life and you're not funding your future, choosing to stay stagnant. Your forecast is the *key* in making sure you're able to put your money in the right places for you today and for the you in the future.

> "The plan is how you get things done in life!"

Follow the Budget

So, you've set money aside for some funds and for the plan. Now what do you do with the plan money? It's simple; you spend it on your Wish/Risk list. You should have a living document of all your wish items and your major risks, meaning you continually update your list throughout the year. Any major risks in life such as big debts must be listed on the Wish/Risk list. This is also where your wish list goes. That new TV, or down payment for the new car, that all comes from the plan. The more money you can set aside for the plan, the better you can invest in your future. As long as you follow your budget and do not overspend in any area your plan will be protected.

However, if you overspend in expenses, funds, or any bills, the money you overspent must come from the plan. In short, when you spend more than you can today you're stealing from your future. The purpose of this section, make sure you follow your budget.

How do you get the new experiences or fun toys you want out of life?

Follow Your Schedule

Once you get a hang of how much money you can spend on expenses per day, set the right values in your funds, and have money set aside for your plan, your budget is going to run smoothly. You'll also notice your credit score will continually slowly raise. At this point you no longer have to worry about your costs, your short-term risks, or how you will fund your future, simply because you follow your budget. However, the system that you're building to get you to where you want to go is not just a budget. Remember we built a schedule in chapter 2. You must follow your schedule so you're continuously growing and meeting your objectives. If you slip on your responsibilities on your schedule you're simply taking longer to get to where you want to go. Having the budget, plan, and funds in place isn't enough; a schedule must be followed.

Saving For Retirement

Independence

As previously mentioned, there are two moments in your life when you will need others to take care of you. The first 15-20 years after you're born, most of us require assistance financially. Additionally, for those who make it to retirement you're typically not working full-time. At this age in life, unless others are taking care of you, you have to live off of the money you've been saving throughout your lifetime. When we're young we don't necessarily care about retirement because we have a misconception that it's something we don't have to worry about. However, reality is much different for many. As we age health costs typically increase. Even with good insurance there are typically always co-pays. You want to make sure you can be as independent in your later years of life as you were throughout your life. So be sure to plan accordingly for retirement.

If you don't save, how will you support yourself in your later years of life?

Time Value of Money

Another important detail to keep in mind is that the money you're making today is worth a lot less in the future. There's a concept called the time value of money. It's the idea that money today is worth more than money in the future due to inflation or its buying capacity. There's even an equation for you to figure out details; but depending on your mathematical skills it may be slightly difficult. The important thing you need to know about the time value of money is the value of a dollar changes dramatically depending upon when you receive it and what you do with it. This is one of the reasons the cost of living increases each year. What it will cost you in the future to retire will be a much more than what things cost you today to make ends meet. So, it's important you make sure you have enough money available for retirement.

How much do you want to have available each year of retirement?

401(k)
Although there are many ways to get prepared for retirement, such as investments throughout life or saving each year, one way that many have available to them is a 401(k). Many companies will match what you contribute to your 401(k). Put simply, this is free money you're choosing to give up if you do not invest into your 401(k). Make sure if your company does any type of matching for 401(k) you get enrolled in that program. It's a nice way to ensure you have extra money for retirement. Like mentioned before, there's many ways to get prepared for retirement. If you're not aware of any resources be sure to Google and locate some; there are many available.

Chapter Three Summary - Money, a Rare Resource

The Big Picture
First off, congratulations on finishing this chapter; it's not an easy read. Let's get out of the weeds for a second and review what we've learned thus far in the book, at a high-level. We first taught you your emotions will sabotage your future if left uncheck, learn emotional intelligence. You then learned you're in the driver seat; you can go wherever you're willing to go. Meaning, if you're not where you want to be in life, only you can change that – you've got to step it up, be an adult, and make it happen. Then we taught you not only are schedules needed, but they also must be protected as if it were your own health, because it is your planned future's health. This is a critical piece to being successful and accomplishing your life goals. You will need a schedule, and it has to be followed and managed. Finally, we covered the hardest of all the secrets to master, following through with your system. Deciding on a path to travel, creating a schedule, and creating a budget is all a waste of time if you don't utilize it all as your system for success; you have to follow-through if you want to achieve goals.

The Budget

In this chapter, we concentrated on walking you through the various areas of the budget. We showed you that if followed, you can budget to manage not only your short-term and long-term goals, but your wish list of wants as well. This chapter's actions will walk you through how to create your budget customized for you. Remember, your budget is how you're going to pay for your trip through the skyscraper of life so you can achieve all your dreams. As you learned earlier, it typically costs money to get to where you want to be, and that's one objective of the budget. We utilize a schedule to manage your time to achieve goals, and a budget to manage your money to ensure you can financially survive, while funding your schedule. Remember, the two are interconnected and both equally critical. One will fail without the other. As a reminder, the second objective of a good budget is to continually maintain or increase your credit score. We'll cover in the next chapter all the details about your credit score and how the system and budget we're building together accomplishes the second objective.

Areas of the Budget

You learned that each of the budget items fall into one of three buckets, either daily tasks, weekly tasks, or monthly tasks. In the monthly tasks you have the debt, credit card, and forecast management sections of the budget. For daily and weekly tasks, you have tracking your income, costs, and spending. Below is a quick reminder of what the purpose of each section is:

- **Monthly Task: Debt Management** – You're in control, so act like it. Don't hide behind the "ignorance is bliss" bug and ignore your debt. This simply ruins your credit score. Be sure you at least have a clear understanding of what debt you have.
- **Monthly Task: Credit Card Management** – Everyone should have multiple credit cards (i.e., more than 5) and you should get a credit card as early in your life as possible. We all should be utilizing credit card rewards to make extra money. Doing this is simple; ensure you have no minimum payments or interest payments by paying off anything you put on your credit cards within 30 days.
- **Monthly Task: Forecast** – Unlike the Debt and Credit Card areas of the budget, the Forecast is a working tool. It's critical that all of your monthly costs are tracked in a meaningful way. You first must calculate your after-tax income – the amount of money you make after taxes are taken out of

your check. With this number you're able to divide it up into three chunks, 50%, 30%, and 20% of your income. Your essential costs or needed items should never be more than 50% of your total after-tax income for the month. All of your "wants" should not exceed 30% and 20% of your after-tax income should be spent on saving for retirement and repaying debts.

- **Daily/Weekly Task:** For your daily and weekly tasks you need to track your income, costs and spending. By using only credit cards for all purchases, it makes it really easy to track spending and costs for any expenditures. This is important so you don't have to spend much time managing your budget. You want to ensure every reoccurring monthly payment is setup on auto-pay. For your daily spending, utilize one credit card with rewards, if available, to use for expenses – or your daily spending for food and entertainment. Separating all bills onto one card and all expenses onto another allows for an easy way to track that all bills were paid and the amount spent on daily expenses was within budget.

Funds & The Plan

After covering the key areas of the budget, we discussed the importance of making more money year-over-year to feed your funds and the plan. Remember a fund is when you take a subset of money and set it to the side to use for a particular purpose. We utilize funds to manage our short-term risks. The plan is how you get things done. Any long-term risks or wish list items are managed via the plan. However, unless you can set money aside for the plan, those long-term risks go unmanaged. Additionally, we expressed the importance of preparing for retirement so you can realize the same independence in your later years of life. We reminded you that money saved today will be worth less in the future so prepare accordingly.

Chapter Three Action – Your Budget

Chapter Three has one of the hardest action sections. Chapter one's action was to get you thinking about your future that you have control over. Chapter two's action was to create a long-term schedule, some milestones for you to reach. In this chapter we will be creating three key areas of your system and budget: your forecast, debt, and credit card management sections. This will allow you to understand your financial landscape – which is critical to create a plan.

Part 1 of 3: Debt Management

It's best to group your debt based on whether it's good or bad debt. Below you'll see an example of how you should structure your debt. Remember, for each item of debt you should list the following: Debt name, Debt Amount, and if you're making monthly payments, the Debt Monthly Due Dates and Monthly Payment Amount. Using the example below, please create your own version of the debt management section, only stretching out for all 12 months in the year. Keep in mind this should be looked at and updated monthly.

Debt Name	Monthly Payment	Monthly Due Date	January Balance	February Balance	March Balance
Collections Bill #1	$150	23	$8,000	$7,850	$7,700
Collections Bill #2	Not paying at present		$13,000	$13,000	$13,000
Car Loan	$315	15	$17,356	$17,041	$16,726
Mortgage	$900	1	$64,789	$63,889	$62,989
Student Loans	$450	22	$95,000	$94,550	$94,100
TOTAL	$1,815		$198,145	$196,330	$194,515

Part 2 of 3: Credit Card Management

Credit cards are our tool for paying our monthly bills, tracking our spending, and making income. Remember, your credit card section should have the following information for each credit card: Credit card name, its monthly due date, its current minimum payment, the credit limit, the current balance, amount of rewards, and how much you paid in interest for that month. This area should also be updated monthly. If ever a credit card is higher than expected, you'll need to understand why, correct what caused it to be too high, and plan accordingly. Please create yourself a credit card management tool in either Excel or using pen and paper. Utilize the example on the next page to create your own, only being sure to add each month of the year.

Credit Card Name	Due Date	Credit Limit	February				
			Minimum Payment	Interest	Total Costs	Rewards	Current Balance
Capital One MC	13	$3000	$75	$27	$102	$8	$2,760
Chase Visa	10	$5,000	$0	$0	$0	$0	$0
Citi Card	15	$1,000	$17	$4	$21	$2	$450
Macys	26	$2500	$0	$0	$0	$0	$0
Target	20	$3,000	$25	$2	$27	$15	$246
TOTAL		$14,500	$117	$33	$150	$25	$3,456

Part 3 of 3: Monthly Forecast

The forecast is the backbone to your budget. We utilize the 50/30/20 method to track costs in our forecast as it's simple and widely used. First, you must calculate your after-tax income. After-tax income is the amount of money you make after taxes are taken out of your check. Determine how much money you made per month, for the last two or three months – again, after tax income. If you work in an industry with tips, you simply add all of your cash received with your after-tax income from your checks. Once you've determined your monthly after-tax income, list all of your monthly costs, in the 50/30/20 buckets as explained earlier in the chapter. We provided an example of a populated forecast on the next page for you to mimic. Feel free to utilize Excel or pen and paper to create your forecast. Just remember, this is a monthly budget task so you should come back and update your forecast each month, after updating your debt and credit card sections of your budget.

In each of the three areas of the example forecast (i.e., Lifestyle Choices, Essential Expenses, and Financial Priorities), you'll notice each area has two items in bold above the total. These are items that everyone should have on their forecast (i.e., funds, The Plan, credit card minimums, expenses, retirement and savings). Additionally, you'll notice on the same row as the total is a percent (e.g., in the Lifestyle Choices section is reads 23%). You get this number by taking the total of that section, and dividing it by your after tax income (e.g., in the Lifestyle Choices section, $1,772 / $7850 = 23%). Remember, you want this percent to equal what that section should be (e.g., Lifestyle Choices should be 20%).

Lifestyle Choices (30%)		Personal, voluntary and often fun choices about how you spend your discretionary income	
Name of Cost	Due	Amount	Paid By
Massage Envy	13	$110	Capital One
ADT Security	10	$51	Capital One
Internet/Cable	15	$146	Capital One
Netflix	26	$15	Capital One
Funds	30	$700	Chase Card
The Plan	30	$750	Chase Card
TOTAL		**$1,772**	**23%**

Essential Expenses (50%)		Expenses you need in order to maintain the fundamentals of your life	
Name of Cost	Due	Amount	Paid By
Utility Bill	1	$150	Bank Account
Cell Phone	26	$250	Capital One
Rent	1	$900	Bank Account
Car Insurance	29	$175	Capital One
Credit Card Min	30	$400	Bank Account
Expenses	30	$2,000	Chase Card
TOTAL		**$3,875**	**49%**

Financial Priorities (20%)		Goals that are essential to a strong financial foundation	
Name of Cost	Due	Amount	Paid By
Student Loans	13	$439	Bank Account
Car Payment	10	$550	Bank Account
Loan Payment	15	$850	Bank Account
Credit Card Costs	30	$100	Bank Account
Savings	30	$250	Bank Account
TOTAL		**$2,189**	**28%**

Forecast Summary	50/30/20 Analysis	
Monthly Income	Monthly Costs	Variance
$7,850	$7,836	$14

Chapter 4
Managing Credit & Financing

"It's not the load that breaks you down. It's the way you carry it."

- Lena Horne

Introduction

In chapter one you learned you're in the skyscraper of life, ignorantly in the driver seat of your future. If you're not where you want to be it's because you haven't chosen to be there. I strongly feel anyone reading this truly gets chapter one because you're still guiding yourself towards success by reading this book. In chapter two you learned that every organized entity uses schedules because they work, and that you should utilize a schedule for any major goals you have in life. Once your schedule is created you must protect your schedule's health as if it were your own health, because it is your planned future's health. In chapter five we'll complete your chapter two action and create your short-term schedule, as well as stress again the importance of following through with your schedule.

In chapter three you learned the various parts to the budget and why it's absolutely necessary for you to utilize a budget to manage your income and costs. You also built out each piece of your budget, with your own unique details. In this chapter we're going to concentrate on how to manage each section of your budget to support your overall vision on where you want to be in life. However, before we get into managing the budget we want to talk about your credit score. As you learn how to manage each section of the budget you'll realize many sections concentrate on keeping your credit score either where it currently is or growing. In order to understand how the budget does this, it's important you first understand credit and how your credit score is calculated.

Credit Score

What is a Credit Score?

It's important everyone understands credit. Ironically, if you randomly ask a person to define "credit score," many struggle to accurately articulate what it is. So, let's start there, defining what a credit score is. A credit score is a number assigned to a person that indicates to lenders a person's credit worthiness, or ability to repay a debt. It's a three-digit number from 300-850; the higher the score the more responsible a person is considered to be at managing their credit. Your credit score will determine how much you pay in interest, and what awesome deals you're eligible for. This is huge, like the difference between paying $650 a month for your mortgage payment or $1,300 a month – your credit score is that powerful! So, it's imperative you protect and nurture your credit score. The thing is, you won't realize the amazing benefits of having good credit until later in life. Due to the "ignorance is bliss" bug most young individuals aren't aware of this important fact. The result, many people in their twenties don't care about their credit score and ultimately are ignorant as to how their credit works. Since this is a huge part of your life, let's break down the various pieces of your credit score to ensure you understand not only how it's calculated, but how to maintain and increase your credit.

> "Once you understand credit, you can control it!"

What Goes on a Credit Score?

Your credit score is made up of five components, each having a different effect on your credit. Each of these components reviews and analyzes the items on your credit report in different ways. In the coming sections we'll get into the detail on each of the five components and how they look at your credit. But first, let's talk about what types of items will show up, and not show up, on your credit report.

Many people ask me if their cable bill or cell phone bill will show up on their credit report because it's 30 or 60 days late. The short answer is no. Your credit report consists of accounts which all of your debt fall under. There are only four types of accounts you'll find on your credit score. The first is revolving credit such as credit cards or department cards. The second are installment loans such as mortgage loans, student loans or auto loans. Third are public records which are typically only bankruptcies, tax liens from not paying taxes, or a civil judgement from a result of a lawsuit. Finally, the fourth type of account you'll find on your credit score is a collection account. These are created when an account becomes seriously past due and the creditor has to sell the debt to a collection agency. So, using the example from earlier, if your cell phone or cable bill goes unpaid for a prolonged period of time and is sent to a collections agency, then yes it will show up on your credit at that time. However, collection accounts are very bad for your credit so you should avoid them at all costs. Now that we know what types of accounts will show up on your credit, let's look at how these accounts are analyzed.

On Time Payments

As mentioned in the previous section, your credit score is made up of five components, each having a different effect on your credit. Three of the areas make up 80% of your credit score. Those are the areas we're going to dive into. However, we will still talk briefly about the other 20% to ensure you have a holistic understanding of credit.

Let's start with the component that has the biggest impact on your credit, how well you deal with payments on current accounts or debts. This component makes up roughly 35% of your credit score. One of the most important objectives of a budget is to ensure that none of your debts, such as credit cards and loan payments, are ever late. In this chapter's action section you'll go through the steps of managing your budget. One of these steps is to ensure all your bills are setup on auto payments and were paid monthly. By doing this you ensure none of your payments will ever be late. Summed up, you ensure 35% of your credit score will always be positive and moving in the right direction.

"Having bad credit will cost you money and time, two limited resources."

Debt to Credit Ratio

The second most impactful area to your credit is your debt to credit ratio. Put simply, this is a percentage that tells you how much of your available credit you are currently using. For example, if you had one credit card with a $1,000 spending limit and you bought a $200 item, the balance on that card would be $200. So, your credit to debt ratio would be 20% - as $200 is 20% of $1,000 (i.e., $200 / $1,000 = .2 or 20%). If you have multiple credit cards you do the same exercise only adding them all together. For example, you would add all of the credit limits together; then you would add all the balances together; and finally, you would take the balances all added up and divide them by the credit limits all summed up. This concept may seem confusing, but we will go into much more detail later in chapter 4. At present, all you need to know is that you want to get your credit as high as possible while keeping your debt as low as possible. The better you can do this the more you'll control this 30% of your credit score.

Do you know how to increase your credit quickly?

Credit Length

The third most impactful component of your credit score is your credit length. This is calculated by taking the average age of all your credit cards. For example, if you had only two credit cards, one for ten years and one for five years, then your average credit length would be 7.5 years. To get an average credit length, add the years together and then divide that by how many cards you have. In the above scenario you would add the years together, 10 yrs. + 5 yrs. = 15 yrs. Then divide the 15 by how many cards you have, 15 yrs. / 2 cards = 7.5 years for average credit length.

The longer your credit length the better it is for your overall credit score. This area of your credit score makes up roughly 15% of your score. However, there are a few techniques to make your credit length seem much higher than it actually is. One of these is to have someone older than you who has had established credit longer than you, add you onto one of their credit cards. For example, if you have a mother who has had a credit card for 20 years and she adds you to her credit card, that will help your average credit length out quite a bit. Now, I know the thought of you having access to one of your mom's credit cards is scary to your parents, which is why you can simply shred up the credit card after you're added to your parent's credit card. Remember, the purpose of being added to the credit card is so that your credit length is improved so that your credit score goes up; it's not so that you have access to their credit card and their money.

Credit Mix and New Credit

The other 20% of your credit comes from the particular mix of your credit you have at the time, and any new credit inquires, 10% each. Your credit score takes into account the type of credit you have. Meaning, it looks good to have a mix of items on your credit score, such as mortgage loans, student loans, a mix of credit cards, department cards, etc. However, it's not good to have credit accounts you don't intend to utilize. Typically, if you don't use a credit line in some time it gets decreased or removed. Both of these actions are harmful to your credit. To manage this 10% of your credit (i.e., the mix of your credit you have) ensure you keep multiple types of credit.

Your new credit inquiries make up the other half of the remaining 20% of your credit score. To calculate this portion of your credit score it looks at how long it has been since you last opened a new account and how many new accounts you have applied for recently. If you've applied for, or opened, many new accounts this will harm your credit score. The assumption being that there's a high probability you're planning to take on debt, or experiencing cash flow issues. A good rule of thumb to follow concerning credit inquiries is to not exceed more than six or seven credit inquiries in a 12-month period.

Financial Stability

What exactly is a Financial Plan?

Now that you understand what a credit score is and its importance let's change gears to talk about how you're going to gain financial stability and more independence. In chapter two's action you made a high-level schedule, that can't come to fruition without financial support. In chapter three we covered the basic components of a budget and setup a way to manage your risks and protect your credit score. But here's the thing, your schedule and budget will fail without the proper management. For that reason, later in this chapter we'll get into detail around how to manage each area of your budget and schedule accordingly. But you need to understand what a financial plan is to understand why you're managing each piece.

To be successful in your life goals you absolutely have to manage your personal finances. The biggest problem most people have with this is they don't know exactly what a financial plan is, and certainly have no clue about the specific segments the plan should cover. A financial plan is much more than just tracking your income, costs, and managing a budget. A financial plan is a comprehensive evaluation of your current and future financial state. Your financial plan has to align with, and help you achieve, your life goals. Financial plans don't have a specific format. However, the good ones support and fund your life goals, ensure you're covered for retirement, and are fluid with updates on a regular basis.

The Components of a Financial Plan

In this section we're going to cover most of the components that a good financial plan should have. I say "most" because again, if you have the financial stability to invest in multiple assets and need assistance with fall back plans for your investments, then this book isn't for you. We're covering all the components necessary to get someone to success.

- Financial Goals: The basis of your financial plan is your clearly defined financial goals, including money for your funds and plan (e.g., college education for your children, buying a larger home, starting a business, retiring on time or leaving a long-term job). The milestones for your financial goals should align 100% with your schedule milestones created in chapter two's action section.
- Analysis of Cash: Your financial plan should include an income and spending plan that defines how you'll afford current costs as well as debt repayment, savings and investing each month. The forecast you created in the action section of the previous chapter allows you to manage this portion of your financial plan.
- Retirement Strategy: Your plan should include how you plan on achieving retirement, specifically independent from all other financial priorities. It should detail out how you'll accumulate the required amount of assets for retirement, and your plan to fund it throughout your lifetime. For now, we have you reserve a spot on your forecast for savings. However, once you're financially stable. be sure to plan out retirement in more detail.
- Risk Management Plan: This section of your plan is to identify all risks to you and your family and provide the necessary coverage to protect your assets against financial loss. We'll talk about risk management in more detail later in this chapter. Funds in your forecast are meant to fund your short-term risks, and The Plan is to fund your long-term risks. Once you're more financially stable it's important to also include items such as life and disability insurance, personal liability coverage, property and casualty coverage, and catastrophic coverage.

How do you want to spend your money?

As stated before, when you become more financially stable you'll want to add more sections to your financial plan. One of those areas is a tax reduction strategy to identify ways to minimize taxes you must pay. The law allows many ways to save on taxes, and the more money you make the more important this area becomes. You'll also want to create an estate plan. An estate plan is just a fancy way of saying to ensure you have arrangements for your belongings when you pass away – no one lives forever so plan for your death. Ensure you have a will, power of attorney, and medical directives.

Managing the Forecast to Feed the Plan

Now that we've explained how your credit score is determined and the criticality of a financial plan along with its various components, we want to segue back to how you should manage each section of your budget to support your overall vision on where you want to be in the skyscraper of life. We are going to start with your forecast. You should also pull up your own forecast as you read this section.

Recall, that updating your forecast is a monthly task when it comes to managing your budget. So, the steps we are about to cover should be performed at the end of each month. Also, if you recall the analysis of cash section of your financial plan, your forecast is also how you'll ensure you can afford current costs as well as debt repayment, savings and investing in your future each month.

There are three steps to updating your forecast monthly. First, you must review each section for accuracy. Each cost should be reviewed to ensure its amount and the card that pays it is accurate. Also, check your math! The second step to updating your forecast monthly is to balance your forecast. In this step you review all the costs that vary month over month like funds, the plan, expenses, utility bills, etc. You want to ensure you have the accurate amounts listed on your forecast.

Finally, the third and last step is to calibrate your forecast. In this step you review each section to ensure you're spending the correct percentage of your income in that section (i.e., 50/30/20 rule). If you find you're spending more than you should in a particular section you need to brainstorm ways to lower spending in that category. In the Lifestyle Choices section that may mean getting rid of a luxury like Netflix. For Essential Expenses it may be finding cheaper car insurance. And for Financial Priorities you may need to refinance your vehicle to get a lower monthly payment.

The Vision

Why The Plan is Critical

So, let's say after a few months you've calibrated your forecast and each of your three sections are as they should be, 50/30/20 percent. We know where all the bills listed came from, or we should that is. We know that funds are the set amount of money put aside to pay for your short-term risks (i.e., anything you absolutely need on a monthly basis). But as we covered earlier in the book, the plan is how you get things done. The plan is how you fund your Wish/Risk list. This is the list everyone's always creating but never does. Mainly because they haven't mastered the skill of the fourth well-guarded secret, following through is critical to success. But for the vast majority they can't afford everything they put on their list. That's why having money set aside for the plan is critical.

Why is your Wish/Risk list so critical?

Wish/Risk List

Your Wish list is getting you those wish items you've always wanted like that vacation in Hawaii, New York, Las Vegas, or Orlando; the new vehicle you've needed or the home you've been dreaming of. These things are not beyond your reach once you begin funding your plan. The Vision is what we call the part of your customized tool that manages your plan of Wish/Risk items. In this chapter's action section in addition to practicing balancing out your budget, you'll be building your plan. The second part of your Vision will be how you schedule your personal growth to get you where you want to be in the skyscraper of life. But we'll cover that portion in chapter five when we get into project management. For now, know that the plan is how you can obtain your wish items. Now, let's talk about the Risk portion of your Wish/Risk list.

Your risks are the items in life that will cause you to have higher monthly cost per month or hurt your credit score. For example, if you don't pay your car insurance off in full for six months you end up paying a little more and having a monthly bill on the forecast. This is a risk you should manage so that you can have it paid off in full when possible. The credit card debt you owe, it's costing you interest; it's a risk. Any debt that's in the thousands, how are you planning to pay it off? That's a risk. Most people know the financial risks in their life. They're the things that make you uneasy about your finances at night. The plan is how you manage these risks so they don't fill your life with stress – when you should be working on you and your future.

Managing The Risks

You Are the Biggest Risk

Managing your major long-term risks via the plan and short-term risks via funds is a necessity, but there are also other risks that neither your funds nor the plan manages. That's your daily management of income, credit, and debt. It's the managing of you. The reason why we spent the majority of the book on the first four secrets is because they are around managing you, the steps to self-growth.

The first rule, self-awareness: you're in the driver seat; you're in control of your future. Some things in life are uncontrollable, but for everything else, it's on you to achieve success – no one owes you anything. If you're not where you want to be in life do something about it!

The second rule, self-understanding: you must learn emotional intelligence extremely well if you want to be successful in life. Without emotional intelligence you do what you feel like at that time, and only think short-term. This will ultimately hinder or prevent your long-term goals and success. Understand emotions so you can control yours.

The third rule, self-planning: you must protect your schedule's health as if it were your own, because it is your planned future's health. Think about where you were in life five years ago. Imagine if you chose a different more informed/productive path than what you chose. How much could it have helped you out today? Now, imagine yourself in five years; you can ensure the you in five years has a better life than the you today. A schedule is your map to success; without it you will fail. Learn how to schedule well!

The fourth and hardest rule to follow, self-control: following through is critical to success, especially when creating and following your system. Having a perfect schedule and budget to fund that schedule is absolutely pointless if you don't follow both, thoroughly. The short-term scheduling in chapter five will help you with this a lot.

This section is meant to share an important piece of wisdom. **The fifth well-guarded secret about life is that you are your biggest risk in life.** You can find coaches, mentors, or books to help you be successful – as you're doing now. However, if you don't have the self-discipline and care enough about your goals to follow through with you plans, all your planning, learning, etc. was all for nothing. You are your biggest risk. Understand that, and utilize our techniques to manage yourself.

Managing your Debt

Now that we've covered how to manage your forecast and the risks associated, let's switch gears to talk about how you maintain the debt section of your budget. Recall, this section simply lists all your debt, and what the balance was at the end of each month. Please grab the debt portion of your budget you made in the previous chapter. As you'd imagine, managing this portion is simple. At the end of each month you simply list for that month the balance of every debt. Remember, the elimination of debt is a risk managed by The Vision. In this chapter's actions we'll create your Vision.

Managing your Credit

The final area of your budget created in chapter three is the credit management section. To manage this section each month you must perform three tasks. First, you must list what you paid for a minimum payment, interest, and what the current balance is for each credit or department card. You also need to list the total cost and how much you have in rewards for each card. The second task is to verify the credit limit is the same. You should also keep track of the last time the credit limit was increased. You should request a credit increase each year to help improve your credit score. Finally, the last step is to update the credit card minimum on your forecast based on what the total credit card minimum cost was. Below is an example of a populated credit management section.

Credit Card Name	Due Date	Credit Limit	February				
			Minimum Payment	Interest	Total Costs	Rewards	Current Balance
Capital One MC	13	$3000	$75	$27	$102	$8	$2,760
Chase Visa	10	$5,000	$0	$0	$0	$0	$0
Citi Card	15	$1,000	$17	$4	$21	$2	$450
Macys	26	$2500	$0	$0	$0	$0	$0
Target	20	$3,000	$25	$2	$27	$15	$246
TOTAL		$14,500	$117	$33	$150	$25	$3,456

Managing Daily Life

Now that we covered how to manage the monthly management areas of your budget, let's now talk about the daily/weekly items. Your daily responsibilities are actually quite simple. Do not spend cash, use credit cards for everything feasible. If you have multiple cards, use one for the auto payment for your bills. Use another for your expenses, and use a third for your fund items. It's a nice way to ensure three cards are constantly getting usage. It also makes it much easier for your weekly tasks.

Weekly, you simply log into your credit cards online to look at what you spent on expenses, plan items, and funds. By doing this each week you ensure you do not spend over your weekly allowance in each bucket. At the end of the month you add up all the weeks and determine if you stayed within budget If not, figure out why and correct the root cause so it does not derail you again.

Chapter Four Summary – Managing Credit & Financing

Chapter four served as the glue to connect what we've been learning up to this point. We started with grounding you in what a credit score was along with what goes on your credit report and how those accounts are analyzed in the 5 components to define your credit score. We then covered in detail what a financial plan is, expressing how critical it is that you have one in your life. We then shared the key components of a financial plan to show you that by following the actions in this book you've created yourself a financial plan.

Next, we went into managing the three areas of your budget created thus far in chapter three. We started with your forecast, introducing the last area of your budget you'll be creating, The Vision. This section is the part of your customized system that manages your plan of Wish/Risk items. We discussed what your Wish/Risk list is and the importance of managing your risks. We talked about your biggest risk being you.

Finally, we closed the chapter off with how to manage your debt and credit sections of the budget. Additionally, we covered how to manage your spending and weekly review of your spending to ensure you can successfully manage your spending to support your forecast.

Chapter Four Actions – The Vision: Your Plan

This chapter's action has two parts. The first is to practice balancing the three areas of your budget as described in this chapter. There are weekly and monthly tasks you should be practicing. You should also set an alarm in your phone to go off at the end of each week, reminding you to do your weekly or monthly balancing of your budget.

The second ask in this action is for you to build the portion of your system that will help you manage your plan. Now, some of you are unable to put any money in your plan today. However, you should still create this section for when you get some cash to put into the plan each month. Below you'll find an example of the layout you should build. In this example this individual has $200 a month in their forecast for the plan – this is why you see a budget for $200 each month. Your Wish/Risk items go below the budget for each month. The "Spent" listed at the bottom of each month lets you know how much you have spent that month, and "Saved" informs you how much you've saved holistically amongst various months up to that month.

January		February		March		April	
$200	Budget	$200	Budget	$200	Budget	$200	Budget
-$100	Save	-$200	Save	-$500	Pay Debt	-$200	Save
-$100	Shoes						
$100	SPENT	$0	SPENT	$500	SPENT	$0	SPENT
$100	SAVED	$300	SAVED	$0	SAVED	$200	SAVED
May		June		July		August	
$200	Budget	$200	Budget	$200	Budget	$200	Budget
-$200	Save	-$200	Save	-$800	Insurance	-$200	Save
$0	SPENT	$0	SPENT	$800	SPENT	$0	SPENT
$400	SAVED	$600	SAVED	$0	SAVED	$200	SAVED
September		October		November		December	
$200	Budget	$200	Budget	$200	Budget	$200	Budget
-$200	Save	-$200	Save	-$800	Black Fri	-$200	Christmas
$0	SPENT	$0	SPENT	$800	SPENT	$200	SPENT
$400	SAVED	$600	SAVED	$0	SAVED	$0	SAVED

Chapter 5

Next Steps in Life, Achieving Goals

"Most people fail in life because they major in minor things"

- Tony Robbins

Accomplishing Goals

Why we don't Accomplish Goals?

If you were to Google why people don't accomplish goals you'll get various responses like the goal was too vague, poor tracking of goals, a loss of focus, lack of planning, etc. You'll get a long laundry list of reasons. I don't necessarily disagree with all of those answers; I just feel there's an easier answer. People fail to accomplish goals because they don't understand what a goal is and how to manage one. Getting you where you want to be in the skyscraper of life will require you being an expert at accomplishing your goals. For that reason, we're going to start by defining what a goal is and breaking it down to its various pieces.

A good goal must be planned for.

Breaking a Goal Down

Depending where you look a goal's definition varies slightly. However, holistically the premise is the same no matter where you go. A goal is the entity of a person's ambition or effort; a desired result. Meaning, you want something to change, or occur. But that's on the surface. All goals, when broken down, should have other attributes – depending on the size of the goal. For example, if your goal will take you multiple months to complete, you should have milestones, or short-term objectives you need to complete along the way. If all your objectives/milestones are met, then you ultimately accomplish your goal. Later in this chapter we're going to teach you techniques to help you better manage your goals.

Do you always accomplish your goals?

Goals are simply projects

So, if a goal is something a person is trying to achieve. Then that's no different than a project that companies run all of the time. If all the successful companies out there utilize project management to achieve their goals, why don't you? For most, the answer to that question is, "I don't know project management, at least not officially." So like with goals, let's start by defining what project management is, then break into the details around project management.

Project Management

What is a Project?

A project is a temporary event that has a defined beginning and end date/time. Each project utilizes a specific set of knowledge, processes, skills and tools to accomplish a singular goal. There's no way I can teach you everything about project management in this book. However, there are some key features about projects that if you were to apply to your goals, will allow you to accomplish many more goals. In the next two sections we're going to cover these key processes and teach you how to take your goal and break it down to the multiple pieces it'll take to achieve its objectives.

Everyone should have project management skills

Key Process Areas of Project Management

According to the PMI, the experts on project management, there are over 40 processes that can be utilized to accomplish a project. However, to accomplish your own goals you only require a few. The first is collecting requirements. We know what we want to achieve as an objective. However, this step requires you to truly have a clear view of what you want the end state of your goal to be. For example, if your goal is to get promoted then part of the requirements is for you to fully understand what the role and responsibilities for the position you're seeking consist of. The second is defining deliverables. A deliverable is a tangible or intangible item produced as a result of your project. Using the example above (i.e., trying to get promoted), your deliverables may be an increase in pay, a new title, and an office. What are the outcomes you want from your project? The third is creating your work breakdown structure (WBS). A WBS simply a fancy way of saying each deliverable has multiple objectives that must be met before that deliverable can come to fruition. For example, accomplishing the deliverable of getting an office, one of the steps you may need to do is first understand company policy around who can and cannot get an office. Because this is a critical step, we're going to talk about this in more detail in the next section. The final area is defining the schedule. Once you have a list of your deliverables, along with the multiple tasks or objectives that must be met to achieve that deliverable, you're now ready to schedule it all. Some items on your lists will need to happen before others.

We'll be building a tool to help you with this portion in this chapter's action area.

Did you know what a project was? Can you now define what a project is?

Breaking down Deliverables

In the previous section we talk about figuring out the requirements for each of your goals. From there, defining what are the deliverables you're attempting to achieve. Next is breaking down the deliverables. Before we get into your short-term schedule it's important that you understand how to break down a deliverable. Breaking your deliverables into smaller pieces helps you identify any dependencies and create a timeline to know how long it will take you to accomplish a deliverable.

There are three rules that if followed will make it easier for you to create your work breakdown structure for each deliverable needed to accomplish your goal. First, is that you must include everything needed to accomplish the deliverable in the work breakdown structure. Second, concentrate on outcomes, meaning what you want to happen. When thinking through projects many feel actions are what you're trying to produce here and you're not. You're trying to identify outcomes not actions. For example, if your deliverable is better pay, one of the bullet lists under this deliverable in your work breakdown structure would be to identify salary ranges for the position you're looking at, in your industry and area.

The entire premise of the first part of this chapter is to teach you the sixth well-guarded secret: **to be successful in life you need to be able to accomplish goals, which requires learning the skills to manage goals.**

Short-Term Schedule

What is Success?

Throughout this book we have talked about success. The objective of this guide is to help you get to where you want to be in life. If you accomplish that goal then you're being successful in life. Just as there's no one answer to where everyone wants to go in life, there's no one answer to what is success. It's different for everyone. However, most goals people set require you to be financially stable, requires a schedule for goals, and for the follow through to complete them.

> If you don't manage your biggest risk, you, you will fail!

Schedules – The Road Map

Earlier in the book we created and started to populate your long-term schedule. That schedule consists of your milestones on your way to where you want to be in the skyscraper of life. However, if you don't manage your time well, you won't accomplish those objectives. A short-term schedule is how you ensure that you accomplish the needed tasks, and helps you manage yourself. A good short-term schedule manages from three views, a quarterly, monthly, and daily view. The quarterly view is to ensure we are headed towards the milestones on your long-term schedule. The monthly level helps you complete the quarterly task, and as you guessed it, the daily tasks ensure you meet your monthly goals and manage your daily time.

What is success or failure for you? What's on your long-term schedule?

Building the Journey

Remember you're in the skyscraper of life on a journey to where you want to be. So, your short-term schedule should be designed to represent a journey. It should have a place to capture each monthly goal for the year, and each task needed to accomplish the monthly goals, by the 13 weeks in the current quarter. Later in this chapter's action section we'll create your short-term schedule.

Now that we've covered what goals are and how to manage them via project management, I'd like to switch gears to talk about relationships.

Relationships

What is a relationship?

Again, like many words in the English language, depending where you look you'll get a slightly different definition. That being said, holistically a relationship is the state of being connected. Or as we'll be referencing it, a relationship is the way two or more people or objects are connected. If you have a supervisor at work you must interact with at times, a doctor you go see, friends, family, or enemies, you have relationships. For the vast majority of us we will need to have relationships as we travel through the skyscraper of life. I always envision relationships as a string going from your heart to another's. For a parent or child it's not a string, it's a titanium thick chain that's unbreakable. For friends that you've known for decades it may be the same. For new friends it may be a tough string. Depending upon the type of relationship the string is stronger or thicker. Over time as individuals fade out of our lives sometimes the string is still there, but it's just become thinner as you've grown apart.

Do you know how to nurture a relationship?

Criticality in Managing Relationships

So why are we talking about relationships. It's simple, as you'll have to have many relationships as you travel through the skyscraper of life, it's important you know how to manage them well. Some relationships will mean the difference between meeting an objective or not. Because of this, the seventh well-guarded secret about life is that **you must know how to manage relationships, as they may mean the difference between you accomplishing a goal or not.** Because relationships are so important, we're going to cover one of the biggest factors to a relationship being successful, communication.

You have multiple relationships to manage.

Communication

Communication is the exchange of information. Now there are entire books written on communication. So, like any other skill, you will need to research and learn more about communication to get better at it. However, as it relates to relationships we wanted to touch base on one key area of communication that we feel everyone needs to understand. This area has to deal with the complexity of the scenarios or topics we're communicating about.

Many times, what someone *intends* to communicate isn't necessarily what is *actually* understood by the communication. This is the root of many disagreements in relationships. To overcome this, try to view every topic and situation as an empty table. On that table are all the facts regarding the situation or topic, good and bad. When you're disagreeing, arguing or failing to communicate effectively with someone more times than not, your two tables do not look the same. Either you or the other party has more facts that the other's is missing. Typically, in this situation both sides feel like they have the accurate facts. It's here when you need to remove the complexity in order to better communicate. A great approach is to say something along the lines of, "I understand this to be the scenario (stating brief pertinent facts), and as a result, I feel this way about the topic. Can you help me understand the facts from your perspective so we can be better aligned around the details?" Granted, this will not always work. However, the premise is until you have the details to understand what the other person is trying to communicate, it's very difficult for you to understand and agree with them.

Many situations are more complex than we know.

Active Listening

The final piece we're going to discuss around communication is active listening. Active listening is mindfully hearing such that you can comprehend the meaning of the words being spoken to you. The premise is if you're actively listening to someone you can repeat, in your own words, what was said. When you actively listen to something you're attempting to understand exactly what they're saying. Without actively listening it's very difficult to communicate. If you're busy thinking of your rebuttal or your perspective while someone's speaking to you, there's a high probability that you're not truthfully actively listening.

Empathy

So why did we concentrate only on those two areas of communication (i.e., the need to see situations or scenarios from other perspectives and the ability to actively listen in order to do so)? It's simple, empathy. Empathy is the ability to not only understand, but share others' feelings. Although emotional intelligence plays a big role in this, the ability to understand situations from other's perspective will allow you to show empathy – which is one of many critical skills needed to be successful throughout the skyscraper of life.

External Demeanor

External Presence

The next area we want to dive into is your external presence. As you grow and move higher in the skyscraper of life others will see you as knowledgeable. And they're absolutely correct in thinking so because you are; you know how to get further up the skyscraper of life than them. This is when you should start becoming a mentor. Like any skill, if you don't use it you'll get less efficient with it. It's the same with you growing. By mentoring you begin to understand topics in more detail, helping you to grow more. It also forces you to view a topic more broadly, gaining perspective. Additionally, a mentee can teach you something. The point is there are multiple benefits to mentoring once you've gained knowledge others haven't yet learned in the skyscraper of life. However, to realize some of these benefits it requires mentorship, coaching, some means of you sharing your knowledge. For this reason, the eighth well-guarded secret is that **you have to become a mentor if you want to continue to grow; it's one of the best ways to comprehend something more – allowing you to grow more.** A great way to get started is to try to help a friend or family member do the actions in this book. Teach them what you've learned so they can grow. You'll notice very quickly how powerful the eighth secret is.

When you're in a mentoring role there is some basic understanding around hygiene that individuals will expect from you. As blunt as it may sound, no one wants to be mentored by someone who's got bad body odor, or whose breath smells like they just woke up. I chose those topics because most people feel uncomfortable talking about them, not me. If you smell, I'll tell you – I'd want you to tell me! You should shower daily, and utilize soap and deodorant. Now your breath, that's a complicated topic that most don't understand and really need to.

Do you know how to ensure you have good breath?

Breath

Millions of individuals suffer from bad breath. Everyone is told to brush their teeth twice a day, floss, go see the dentist each year, use mouth wash, etc. However, we never are really told the details of what happens when we don't – at least not in intimate detail. Now let's be real with ourselves. Do you always do all the above things all of the time? I know I don't. When you don't thoroughly do all the above, plaque and tartar will build up on your teeth, on the surface and up under the gums. During your regular dentist visits they can remove these items so you're good to go. Keeping up on the maintenance and continually seeing the dentist on a regular basis will help ensure you have good breath. Now of course, you can eat some foods that will leave your breath not so pleasant. You'll need to freshen up your breath before it smells nice again.

White Tongue

Have you ever stuck your tongue out and noticed it had a white film on it? This occurs when the tiny bumps on your tongue swell up and become inflamed. In between those bumps bacteria, dirt, food, and dead cells can all get trapped. It's all this debris that turns your tongue white. It's not just poor brushing, dry mouth, breathing from your mouth, smoking, alcohol, many things cause white tongue. Because of this it's important that you purchase a tongue cleaner to help keep your tongue clean – brushing it many times won't get it clean enough. Also, using an electric toothbrush will be much more effective than your typical toothbrushes. Just remember, if you have white film on your tongue, your breath doesn't smell fresh. It makes me giggle when I see selfies with someone's tongue out and it's white – I subconsciously wonder if they know what that means and are meaning to show us that they have poor oral hygiene.

Plaque

Earlier we mentioned that plaque constantly builds on your teeth as bacteria are always forming in our mouths. Plaque is a sticky, colorless film of bacteria and sugars. It's also the main reason people get cavities. When you don't get it fully off your teeth daily from brushing, it hardens into tartar. The plaque causes the cavities by shooting acid at your teeth. Eventually the tooth enamel breaks down and you have a cavity. If you don't floss daily, the plaque can also irritate the gums around your teeth which will result in gingivitis. Gingivitis is when your gums are inflamed, red, swollen, or bleed easily when brushing. Personally, this alone should motivate you to brush your teeth twice a day and floss daily. But some of you still won't. As long as you go see the dentist regularly you're okay . This is critical because unfortunately, doing all the right oral hygiene techniques yourself still won't get all the plaque off. You get the vast majority, but it's a necessity to see the dentist regularly. So, if you can't get all the plaque even when you do follow all the rules, what if you don't see a dentist regularly?

How's your oral hygiene?

Tartar

Without visiting a dentist regularly, the plaque you're unable to get daily will turn into tartar . Tartar is a mineral buildup so it's easy to see if it's above your gum line. Typically, the sign you have tartar is a yellow or brown deposit at the gum line or between teeth. Unfortunately, the only way to remove tartar fully is with a professional cleaning at the dentist. The great news is even if you've developed gingivitis on your gums and tartar on your teeth, it is all reversible with professional treatment and good oral care at home. However, untreated gingivitis can advance to bad gum disease. Also, plaque can spread and grow below the gum line. Both causes tissues and bone that support the teeth to break down and get destroyed. As a result, the gums separate from the teeth, forming small pockets - in essence spaces between the teeth and gums where even more plaque falls into. The longer you let this go on the pockets deepen and more gum tissue and bone are destroyed, eventually resulting in teeth becoming lose and needing to be removed.

Why the in-depth lesson on dental hygiene? Simple, the ignorance is bliss bug. Many young individuals treat oral hygiene much like their credit, "I'll worry about that later." Millions don't realize they're walking around with bad breath a few hours after brushing and flossing. Even more don't realize that if they don't go see a dentist yearly, they're slowly damaging their teeth – which cannot be replaced and it's very costly to get fake teeth. For this reason, this is the ninth well-guarded secret: **you must take care of your personal hygiene, specifically your oral hygiene.**

Chapter Five Summary - Next Steps in Life, Achieving Goals

In this chapter we discussed the importance of not only setting goals, but understanding how to manage them if we want to be successful. We looked at how we could utilize project management practices to accomplish our goals. We discussed what success means to you, and why a short-term schedule is critical in managing yourself.

Then we switched gears to talk about relationships. We talked about how you must know how to manage relationships, as they may mean the difference between you accomplishing a goal or not. Finally, we covered the importance of utilizing communication to nurture relationships. We expressed the importance of active listening and utilizing empathy as tools to build successful relationships.

Lastly, we spoke about your external presence. Starting with why you have to become a mentor if you want to continue to grow; it's one of the best ways to comprehend something more. Then we closed out the chapter discussing how you must take care of your personal hygiene, specifically your oral hygiene. As you grow, the expectation is that you know how to maintain good hygiene.

Chapter Five Action – Short-Term Schedule

The action for this chapter has two parts. First, go back to your action created in chapter 2, your long-term schedule. Try to fill more of your schedule out, ensuring that you at least have this year and next year populated. Second, I'd like you to utilize what we spoke about with project management and create your own short-term schedule utilizing the below template. Note, you can and should have multiple tasks per month. You should also be specific in what you call each task.

Quarter One		
January	February	March
Complete Task #1	Complete Task #2	Complete Task #3

Once you've listed all the tasks needed to accomplish your goals for the quarter, put what you will do each week of the quarter. The example below only shows four weeks, but yours should be 13 weeks - listing each task from the monthly planning in the week that you plan on working on it.

	Week 1	Week 2	Week 3	Week 4
Education	Task #1	Task #1		
Career		Task #2		Task #2
Personal Growth			Task #3	

Final Thoughts

The Big Picture

"Take Control of Your Life, Instead of Letting Life Control What You Can Do!"
-Byron B. Townsend

A Guide on How to Get You to Where You Want to Be!

Remember, this book is a guide meant to show you a way to success. Being shown a path is one thing but actually taking the time to grow in the needed skills to get to where you want to be in life is entirely different. I think the saying is, "You can lead a horse to water but you can't make him drink." I can't promise all your issues will be solved by this book. However, I can tell you that you will be more successful throughout life if you accomplish the actions presented to you in this guide. To help you out, we've listed them all below. But before you start checking off what you still have left to do, one last point. As you grow and accumulate knowledge it gives you a few things; access to higher floors in the skyscraper of life, higher pay, and many times you'll learn true wisdom. Just always remember the tenth well-guarded secret, **more success and knowledge doesn't make you better than anyone else; as you grow remember that important fact and stay humble.**

Actions to Complete to Build Your Customized System for Success
- On page nine, write the ten well-guarded secrets
- Learn how you procrastinate & learn emotional intelligence, read a book on both topics
- Complete chapter two's action, your long-term schedule
- Build your budget, the credit card management, debt management, and forecast – following the appropriate steps (which may mean reading back through parts of the guide)
- Get access to your credit score, either through a paid service or a free one like CreditKarma.com. Review the five components of your credit score and understand what's hurting your credit from what we taught you about credit scores.
- Manage your budget, the debt, credit, and forecast areas each month going forward - know your financial landscape and plan
- Utilize project management to create your short-term schedule and update it every two weeks
- Read a book on communication to help you with relationship management
- Take care of your hygiene, especially your breath

Recommendation from the Author

Extra Help

The Real Consultants

"We empower people to change their lives in a dramatic way for the better!"

About Us
    The Real Consultants is a consulting firm that specializes in life, career, and business coaching. We have six locations in the beautiful central Florida area. Our coaches can't wave a magic wand or give you a magic pill to change everything. But, they can help you to look at situations from a different perspective and help you get past the fear that may be holding you back.

    The distance between your dreams and reality is called action. Coaching is about creating an action plan that moves you forward from where you are to where you want to be. That's easier to do when you have someone to guide you who believes in you, encourages you, and gives you valuable feedback. If you feel stuck, lost, unsure what your "thing" is, if you're unhappy, dissatisfied, scared, or just wondering, "now what?" we can help.

Our Services
    We customize each business, career and life coaching package based on your individual needs. Our goal is to provide the package that will work best for you and your situation. However, each plan comes with the following by default:

- A Professional Consultation - We have a free consultation to ensure we can assist you and that we're all on the same page.
- A Scholarly Life Coach - Every Life Coach at The Real Consultants has a Master's degree with real world experience.
- The Vision System - Our proprietary financial, business and life planning tool used to create your customized system for excellence.
- Life Reminders - We send email, text, and voice reminders for important actions, partnering with our clients for success.
- Effective Business Solutions - We utilize the latest Project, Agile, Change, Financial, Cost, and Process Management practices to support our clients.

https://www.therealconsultantsllc.com
CustomerSupport@TheRealConsultantsllc.com | (877) 836-7413

CPSIA information can be obtained
at www.ICGtesting.com
Printed in the USA
LVHW09*1010250818
587966LV00002B/7/P